The Ox and Scorpio

Volume I: Stories For My Sons

M. Chandler

Dear Tom,
You lived something like it you know the struggle. Thank you for lessing my story be a part of yours.
— yours always in friendship —
M. Chandler
GRANDSCORPIO@gmail.com.

P.S. keep writing!

Copyright © 2012 Michael Chandler

All rights reserved.

ISBN: 1475052006
ISBN-13: 978-1475052008

DEDICATION

For my mother whose courage saved me,
For my father whose strength lifts me,
For my children whose promise inspires me,
and
For my wife who gives all of us everything.

CONTENTS

Front Matter

    Acknowledgements   i
    Important Dates   1
    About the Title   3

ACT I   Departure

    Chapter 1   Where We Come From   11
    Chapter 2   My Favorite Things   20
    Chapter 3   Heroes   27
    Chapter 4   The Importance of Leaning   33
    Chapter 5   Manners   37

    Curtain   41

ACT II   Initiation

    Chapter 6   Career   47
    Chapter 7   Art & Beauty   56
    Chapter 8   Knowing God   59
    Chapter 9   Augury and Portent   66

    Curtain   74

ACT III   Return

    Chapter 10   Near Death Parenting   81
    Chapter 11   Uncertainty   87
    Chapter 12   Battle and War   93

    Curtain   107

ACKNOWLEDGMENTS

While this had begun years ago, it would not have seen completion without the support of my wife DeAnn. She believed in the project and in me. While I tackled the bulk of this task she was pregnant with our third child. While I was up late writing this or editing or rewriting a section she didn't complain that I had forgotten to pay her any attention. She waited up for me to come to bed so we could talk about the day though it was near midnight. She read every page of this several times to help me get it right.

My other best friend Eric "Alvie" Alvarez is also partly responsible for this book. Without his constant encouragement, humor and willingness to read numerous drafts and unrelated items to help me carry on it would not have been.

And for all other friends and family who have contributed in their own way to my life and this work, a heartfelt thanks to you all.

Important Dates

1973	Born, Santa Monica California (November)
1974	Arrived Honolulu, on the island of Oahu, Hawaii
1976	Drowned at Honolulu Harbor Pier 21, briefly died
1978	Adopted by L. Frank Aloiau
1979	Saw "Jaws" & became afraid of water, including toilets
1991	Dropped out of James B. Castle High School
1994	Obtained General Education Diploma (GED)
	First attempt at college; Windward Community College
1995	Joined the U.S. Navy
1997	Left the Navy to return to Hawaii
1998	Moved to Washington State (Ellensburg)
1999	Joined Air Force Reserves (on way back into the Navy)
	Worked at Microsoft and moved to Bellevue, WA
2000	Moved to California; first full time civil service position
2001	AAS Degree, Criminal Justice, Comm. Coll. of the Air Force
(pre 9/11)	Moved to Annville, Pennsylvania
	Joined 28th Infantry Division as an Intelligence Sergeant
	Visited my father briefly before he died
2001	Moved to Palmyra, Pennsylvania
2002	Went to Bosnia, met *Alvie*
2003	BA Degree, Leadership, Bellevue University
	Returned from Bosnia and transferred back to Air Force
	Changed name dropping *Aloiau*
2006	Met your mother, bought the *hundred year old house*

Michael Chandler

2007	Married your mother, planned to return to using *Aloiau*
2008	Saw 98% of *Cloverfield*
	Ari arrived
2009	Finally returned to the Navy
	Saw the end of *Cloverfield*
	Moved to Maryland
2010	Forced to buy minivan
	Miranda arrived
2011	Bought the Gettysburg Pool House
2012	Master's Degree, Liberal Studies, Fort Hays State Univ.
	Begin 2nd Volume: *For Panda Said the Ox*

The Ox and Scorpio

About the Title

Originally this work was to be called simply *Stories for my Son*, then as a second son was predicted to arrive just as this was due to be completed, *Son* would become *Sons*. That simply was insufficient as the book is more than stories; it is about our shared past and a distillation of myself, my perspective and orientation. The final title *The Ox and Scorpio* captures that and the subtitle *Stories for my Sons* hints at a focus and purpose.

The *Ox* is first as it represents my father who was born under the same Chinese astrological sign as I. The *Scorpio* is my western astrological sign. Together they represent my mixed heritage; giving me a broad perspective at once occidental and oriental. The use of astrological signs is representative of my mythic orientation and the importance of the invisible unknowable in our daily lives. The conflict that often exists between the east and west or the mythic and mortal realms hinted at by the juxtaposition of the elements alludes to the battles that have raged within me and that I have had to wage with the world.

All of these elements are some of the most important aspects that differentiate me from the more typical central Pennsylvanians of PA Dutch, German or Slavic descent. These are the very basic primal conceptual building blocks of my being. The individual qualities attributed to the *Ox* and *Scorpio* quite accurately describe me, both the positive and the negative. A brief internet search would furnish you with varied lists of those qualities. I would list them here but this should be an interactive experience and like life, require a degree of participation and effort. If that seems like a sinister joke, well I'm a *Scorpio*.

And this brings me to Miranda. The subtitle *Stories for my Sons* is not meant to exclude you, my only daughter. Indeed much of this is intended for you as well. I expect significant blocks of this to be less than fascinating to you and the purpose of using sons vice children or kids is twofold. First, *Stories for my Children* didn't sound right. Second, many of the struggles within me over the course of my life have been a search for validation, a search for my masculinity, a struggle to understand and become what it was my father had intended me to be and to grasp that it did not matter.

I have no experience being a woman or trying to be one and can offer little advice of use to you in the way this work is at least partially intended to help guide my sons should either of them experience moments of doubt or worry about their membership in their gender. I hope to add a volume already taking shape for you specifically – working title *For Panda said the Ox*.

Introduction

Hello son, this book is a compilation of various stories and anecdotes that I hope you enjoy. These stories have been selected to help you know me as well as I would have liked to know my own father. It's intended to provide answers and insight that might benefit you as you make your own way in the world. It is my hope that it may serve as a set of "giant knowledge shoulders" to stand upon if only once. This book also serves as a bridge between *He Was a Ram*, the official Wong Aloiau clan genealogy published in 1985 and you, a bridge to our clan's proud history of humble origin.

To be sure it's not everything I know and want to pass on; I plan to add a volume (or two) in the years ahead. Nor is this intended solely for your use. This is for your siblings as well. This might benefit them as neither has known me for as long as you have, being the first of the brood to have arrived. It is for me too, that I might gain strength and regain focus by revisiting these pages. But it *is for you* as the eldest you will be the guardian of this knowledge and our history; you will help the younger Chandlers to know it.

This work has been taking shape since you were born. You were just beginning to discover words when I was enrolled in Dr. Potts "Ways of Knowing" course at FHSU. He challenged his students to consider the purpose of knowledge. Answering that question seemed to necessitate the writing of this work. That answer is available in my files, but in short my answer is that *"...in part for me to build upon the knowledge and place in the world bequeathed to me by my father that my own children might climb ever higher..."*

This brings me to the organization of this work. I've divided it into three parts or Acts. Act I is about the past, where we came from and my early days, early formative influences and preferences which might be of interest to you as a teenager. There will be some light topical factoids as well. Act II begins with my first foray into the world and might be of interest to you as a young man setting out on your own for the first time. Act III begins with you, it might be most interesting to as you master the world and seek greater mastery over yourself in preparation for the next generation. In each Act it might be evident what state of mind I was in during those times or what kind of man I was but I'll include some reflections at the conclusion of each Act for consideration and to bridge the journey to the next Act.

You already know me as your father and you have your ideas about who I am but you might be wondering what I was like before and how I see myself. I would say I am a self-made man, one who earned everything I have by the sweat of my brow. I am tenacious, having started and started over again with nothing. I'm a man of honor and conscience, a warrior which is to say a man of peace. In my personal dealings with others I have endeavored to be loyal and forgiving, gentle and compassionate. I have tried to be generous placing greater value on shared memories and adventures over possessions or fame.

I defy easy description; it's a curse I've endured throughout my life. A kind of inherited identity crisis which makes knowing my own history difficult. Most folks draw their cultural heritage and identity from their parents. This is difficult for me because I am adopted and for other reasons. I have failed to learn anything meaningful about my biological father so I continue to identify with my adopted father's lineage. It is complex, rich and courageous.

My father's ethnicity and heritage is Chinese, I am thus Chinese but there is a conflicted history in this identity. My father is not "pure" Chinese (of importance only to a part of our clan) and so was himself not always fully embraced and accepted. As a child I was sometimes also rejected by the clan and left to seek an identity that would accept me. Other impure members of the clan dealt with discrimination too, the book *He Was a Ram* was in part intended to heal this rift for others like me of mixed heritage in the clan. It came too late to help me so I just disowned the evil of ethnocentricity expressed by a significant part of the clan. In time they'll come around, or their children will learn the harm caused by such petty evil. It matters not.

To further complicate matters my mother's lineage includes various European national identities and a Jewish tradition. My mother was raised as a Mormon however and so I know nothing of "being (part) Jewish" beyond what I can find on the internet and through attending three services in my life. My father was a member of the Baha'i faith which is of Persian origin, but our Chinese family observed a number of Chinese Folk Religion (Shenism) traditions (deifying important ancestors for example), sprinkled with Lao Tzu's Taoist teachings, Confucianism and Catholicism (from my father's mother Rebecca) as well. So I am also a spiritual orphan.

I'll address each of these facets of our history in a bit as we get further into where we came from. For the moment let us turn to where we are together now as I pen this work for you. It is 2012 and a few months ago we bought the pool house in Gettysburg, Pennsylvania not far from where most of our family was born. You really like it. We're waiting for the youngest member of our family to be born in the spring and we're all very excited about the new baby. My family is a part of who I am, my role as father and husband is far more important to knowing me than how the census bureau might categorize me. Our family, so much a part of me starts with your mother.

Your mother works very hard to take care of us all. She cares for you and Miranda during the day and me in the mornings and evenings. Sadly I work so far away from home I spend more time driving and working than I do with my family each day. I don't get more than a few hours with you so I try to make the most of it. My limited time with you is a source of some anxiety. It reminds me how I worried about my dad leaving for work when I was your age. You are three right now and full of energy, funny questions and imaginative stories but sometimes you are sad that I have to be gone so much.

All in all we're a fortunate family. As a result of hard work and not a little bit of luck we have enough of whatever we need; food to eat, a nice warm house, clothes, toys and we're all happy here in our new place together. Grandma comes to visit a lot and Grandpa some too, even Uncle Pete has been here once. We have good neighbors that bring cookies and smiles. There are no street lights so you can see lots of stars outside in the morning or at night. There are fun things to do and good schools. Your mother and I don't care for the winters and wonder why anyone lives north of the Carolinas but you like the snow that piles up on our front yard and making snowmen with me.

Michael Chandler

ACT I
Departure

Michael Chandler

Chapter 1

Where We Come From

"Distinguished ancestors shed a powerful light on their descendants, and forbid the concealment either of their merits or of their demerits."

-Sallust, Roman Historian

No need for any lengthy explanation here, we hail from Gettysburg, Pennsylvania. You and your mother were born at Harrisburg Hospital just a short trip up Route 15 and across the Susquehanna River. Your Sister Miranda was born south along the same road in Frederick, Maryland and our youngest will be born here. My story is a bit more complicated and begins far, far away.

When meeting new people I am invariably asked "where are you from?" Over the years I've formulated a response "I'm from everywhere really" to avoid an uncomfortable explanation about how stupid I am for moving from Hawaii to Pennsylvania. When you tell people that you are from Hawaii they look at you in a way that says "you're an idiot" while they ask "what brought you to Pee-yaa?"

So where did *I* come from exactly? Not knowing best how to answer this has been a source of significant anguish for me at times. To help you avoid similar confusion in explaining our history to anyone you might care to share this with I'll discuss my own origin and we'll look briefly at your mother's family and their origins as well. I will begin with my beginning, and my father and his side of the family, before exploring the Milletics (Pappy) and Scheffel (grandma) origins.

My Side of the Family

Michael Chandler [1]

    I grew up in Hawaii on the island of Oahu and that probably doesn't mean a lot. You may have heard me say "it's where God goes for vacation" I'm sure you've heard a few stories about how pretty it is but it's also a very crowded and occasionally tense place. There are great racial and ethnic tensions, a significant gap between rich and poor and some less than idyllic areas. There is deep, persistent poverty and serious drug problems. Violent and property crimes occur with a frequency similar to that of a large metropolitan like Detroit or Philadelphia.

    Before high school I lived along the edge of forgotten crumbling industrial areas and Asian immigrant neighborhoods. Those early days in Hawaii were my favorite, before I was aware of how poor we were or how ill prepared I was for my future. Some of my earliest and fondest memories are of the sea lapping gently at the rusted steel sides of a harbor tug tied to pier 21. When I close my eyes I can transport myself there to see, hear and smell the place. Diesel engines at idle, salt, burning oil grease and paint. It was always one of the happiest places for me; there was a promise of adventure and freedom in those boats. I remember that I spent a lot of time with my father there. Usually a trip to pier 21 meant that I was going to be able to spend some time on the sea completely free of the world's concerns.

My Siblings

    I have a half-sister named Leann Aloiau who is my father's daughter by a previous marriage. She lives in San Francisco but I have no contact with her. I never really knew her but I did know my two younger siblings. Monica and Melody grew up with me and I miss them both.

Monica Sui Lin Pi'ilani Castro (maiden name Aloiau)

    The first of my sisters I actually met was Monica. She was born under the sign of the dragon (your little brother is a dragon too!) and like so many of them she was trouble from the start. She was destined for some greatness having the gift of gab and a sharp quick wit. She was a pretty girl but difficult circumstance and cruelty of others altered her trajectory. She became an unwed mother at age 20, a statistic. She was involved with drugs and drug dealers, cruel people with misplaced priorities unwilling to help a teenager with a child of her own. She later married and suffered through a bitter

---

[1] In *He Was a Ram* listed as Michael Chandler Kooney Aloiau under generation 4

divorce. She has had to endure several moves across the country. I called her Nika growing up, we fought a lot. She also fought with the youngest (Melody) – rocky relationships seem to be a recurring theme for her. When you were born she lived in Florida, at the time of this writing she lives in Seattle near but apart from my mother. This is one reason you don't know her. She is a nurse now by trade.

Nika has four children in descending order of age Moira, Keller, Carter and Madison, they are your cousins. I know Moira but only just barely. I knew her when she was a toddler, but that's about it. You have other cousins though who remain as anchors for our branch of the clan in Hawaii.

Melody Kaleo o Nalani Hayase (maiden name Aloiau)

I called her Didi and she was my constant companion. She was frail and delicate of appearance but indestructible in attitude. She was a bit tom-boyish and efficient in her appearance, she never spent the kind of time preening and primping that Nika did. Nika had a keen fashion sense and new clothing; Didi had hand-me-downs and mismatched outfits. She was always smiling and cheerful though and often a little dirty or injured. She laughed at my jokes and always forgave me and my idiot friends' occasional rudeness.

Though they greeted Nika with suspicion and apprehension (she was a dragon after all) my friends accepted Didi as one of the gang despite her being five years junior. The family loved Didi for two. She was born a twin but her sister perished after only five days of life. We never let the love for our sister (Marissa) die, we gave it to Didi and she loved everyone back for both of them too. It's one of the things that make my sister Didi unique and special to so many. She also has the gift of perfect pitch and a terrific voice.

She gives you three cousins in descending order Sean, Marissa and Sarah. Didi and I speak regularly, though less than we'd like to. We used to be in constant contact and she's helped me through some of my toughest times. She is a professional mother and dental hygienist. If you were to visit her she would treat you as one of her own children. She is married to Neil Hayase and they live together in Mililani near the Arizona Memorial at Pearl Harbor.

Grandmother Brenda Gay Aloiau (maiden name Chandler)

While I consider Hawaii home, I was not born there. I was born in Santa Monica California. When I was conceived my mother lived in Utah. She was 16 years old at the time and it was quite the scandal. She was sent to California to stay with foster parents through church social services at her mother's (Sheila Maxfield Kekaula) behest until she gave birth.

Thankfully, my mother refused to consent to an abortion her mother and step-father advocated as a face saving measure for the family and later to her Mother's demands that she and her step-father Eddie Kekaula (a professional musician) adopt me.

This may have contributed to significant distance between me and that side of the family.

Brenda was not welcome back in Utah and so she travelled after my birth and spent some time bouncing around between several relatives. Eventually she moved on to Honolulu on the Island of Oahu. She completed high school and joined the work-a-day world there and soon met my father.

My mother enjoyed painting, she was quite skilled actually and our family homes featured a few of her works in oil on canvas. She was a sharpshooter on her high school junior ROTC rifle team. She was a member of her school and church choirs and high school theatre troupe. She enjoyed singing along with the radio in the car wherever we drove and was a terrible motorcycle rider. She was afflicted with a weak constitution made worse by the strain of the loss of a child and cumulative injuries absorbed over the years.

She worked herself nearly to death at as many as three jobs at once trying to make ends meet so that we would have food and clothes. I remember when times were lean, when my father's job had cut back on sailings she would always find a way to make up the difference. She is a stoic devoted to her family. She sacrificed much of her youth to help raise her eight younger siblings, giving what was left of her youth to her own children.

Later as my sisters and I grew older and more independent she rightly began to reclaim her own life. But when my father most needed her, when he was completely disabled she looked after him until the end without thought for herself.

Grandfather Llewellyn Frank (Hu Chin Wong) Aloiau

My father Llewellyn "Frank" (Hu Chin Wong) Aloiau was a leathery man of *salt* and *iron*.[2] He was a grizzly seafarer of great skill and courage. He was a man's man, of singular integrity even in a time when honor had only begun to go out of vogue in favor of subtle nuance. His voice carried weight,

---

[2] *Salt* as in "an old salt"; a skilled sailor & *Iron* as in spine & will. Also the motto of my own infantry division (the 28th) "Men of Iron".

his words commanded respect and a ferocious temper lurked behind his weathered countenance.

This is not to say he was completely humorless. He could smile, laugh and sing (albeit poorly) carrying on long into the night with his makeshift slack-key musical ensemble in the garage. His steel hands could gently coax masterful compositions of the most complex and gentle quality spontaneously from his favorite guitar, a 1930s vintage Martin & Co. acoustic now lost to time.

He tried to teach me this skill but I never mastered the guitar. I don't know how he did it either. He spent so much time working. He worked himself to death on those tugboats. When I sailed with him he was always alert to his duties, never "lollygagging" and the crewmen always made sure they were busy when he was near or might be.

He didn't care much for those who talked. He was a man of action, his motto: "don't talk– DO!" Yet he enjoyed crossword puzzles, reading and watching Jeopardy. He was something of an enigma that way. Yes he was something of a puzzle at times. His temper for instance could be very unpredictable. He was prone to violent outbursts over silly things like a sock disappearing in the dryer.

The three of us, my younger sisters and I could be quite trying at times so I suppose our antics might be to blame for eroding his patience from time to time. Violence towards children is inexcusable. He was a man of a different time. He was a tough but good dad, sometimes I thought of him as a monster and hated him but it wasn't fair to think of him this way. We are all of us imperfect, he was too and I miss him.

He had many friends, he led his biker gang and he loved motorcycles, trains and horses. He wanted to be a "paniolo" what we call cowboys in Hawaii but World War II came along and he became a soldier, then a sailor. When he returned to civilian life he became a professional sailor as I have always known him.

Great Ancestor Lo Yau Wong[3]

He is the great patriarch of our clan in Hawaii whose life is chronicled in the red book on our shelf titled *He Was a Ram*. He traveled to Hawaii from Canton area (where our people were regarded as barbaric being the last province to join the celestial kingdom).

---

[3] His life is detailed in *He Was A Ram*

He was a bold man, never mistaken for a timid one. Despite official laws in China that forbade working with and traveling amongst the foreigners (English, Dutch, Americans and such) he sought to go amongst them to make his fortune. He narrowed his choices to the Golden Mountains (California) or the Sandalwood Mountains (Hawaii). China was in the throes of revolution and economically stagnant during his youth. Some 30 million Chinese died during the fifteen years of the *Tai Ping Rebellion* immediately preceding his departure for Oahu in 1865.

One of the most important things this bold progenitor passed down was the *importance of learning* (explored in chapter 4), and the importance of land which he believed to be forever (he also loved gold but that didn't get passed down). He built a school in his village on Kauai for the improvised Chinese and Hawaiian children there. He purchased land and set our clan up for success. He was a self-made man, very inspiring to me. I consider myself to be likewise self-made in his style. He arrived in Hawaii with almost nothing, just a suitcase. When I left Hawaii for the mainland I had nothing more than fit in a backpack.

Your Mother's Side of the Family

DeAnn Lynn Milletics

Your mother is the only daughter of Thomas Anthony Milletics originally from the central Pennsylvania area and Carlita (May) Scheffel whose family brought her to Pennsylvania from Bedford, Indiana. Your mother grew up in the Mechanicsburg area and even went to college locally obtaining her Bachelor of Arts degree in social work from Shippensburg University in 2000. She swam in high school and enjoyed a more or less normal childhood. She spent a lot of time with her grandmother Dolores "Nan" and at the community pool where she grew to love swimming.

As a child your mother traveled to Florida sometimes to visit her maternal grandparents who lived there briefly. DeAnn never really lived outside of the Harrisburg area until I dragged her to Frederick MD, which isn't really all that out of the area. Having you come into her life put the importance of family in sharp relief. So we moved back and closer to her clan as soon as we could escape Maryland.

Your mother worked with children most of her life. She taught swimming to little kids, interned at the Mechanicsburg Children's home (at-risk kids) where she took a job after graduation. She also worked with children at Loysville Youth Detention center. When I met her she was working in an elementary school setting with autistic children. She always wanted to work with kids and this was one of the things that initially endeared her to me. She worked right up to just a few weeks of having you.

Your mother also likes hockey, she enjoyed going to Hershey Bears games with her family as a child and we enjoy games together now as adults. On one of our first dates in 2006 we went to a hockey game. We took you and Miranda to one last year (2011) and you two loved it too. We're looking forward to taking you two to another one this coming season. Your mother also loves football. She is an Indianapolis Colt's fan – pending what happens with Peyton Manning who might be traded to my team the Washington Redskins.

One of my favorite things about your mother is that she enjoys cooking and experimenting with recipes as much as I do, no- more. It's manly to cook and know how to take care of yourself by the way. A few tricks with presentation were helpful in wooing your mother. Maybe I'll touch on those in another section. There are a lot of wonderful things about your mother that you might not know; we're going to save most of those for Miranda's book coming later. Your mom is a Scorpio and to some significant degree shares my mythic bent.

Thomas Anthony Milletics

This grandfather you know, he visits infrequently but when he does he lingers and beams with joy at seeing you. He's very proud of you kids. Pappy as he likes to be called enjoys sprint car racing and was on a crew once. He grew up in Enhaut in a house on Mohn Street near our hundred year old house before moving to Mechanicsburg. He bowls with a league in Mechanicsburg and also enjoys hockey and gardening.

He's a jolly hard working fellow who loves to tell long stories that end with a laugh, often there are a few laughs in the middle of his stories too. There doesn't seem to be a cruel bone in him. He has a brother "Uncle Dave" but I don't really know him.

Like my father, Pappy believed in the importance of learning sending your mother to college with money borrowed from his own retirement funds. He worked hard to build that fund and to pay those college bills. He didn't have any easy job; he's a blue collar guy working at the Carnation plant in Mechanicsburg until it moved. He didn't neglect his family though. He made sure his daughter got through school and he was there for his brother and mother when they needed his help too. He kept working.

For his own education he attended the Ambler campus of Temple University to study landscape architecture but was forced to leave college due to a temporary downturn in health. He was never able to return, life happens.

Another interesting fact, Pappy beat polio as a teenager. You might not know what this is; it's a potentially disabling disease that a vaccine was developed for just a few months after Pappy was inflicted with it. Fortunately he did not lose the use of his legs permanently as a result. Ironically, he was a poor runner prior to catching this disease when he recovered he was a faster runner! He played baseball and football throughout high school and was on the track team his senior year.

Dolores Catherine Milletics (maiden name Lucas)

You briefly knew your great-grandmother Dolores (on Milletics side) as "Nan". You visited her regularly with your mother and on holidays, Nan adored you. She was a tough lady who enjoyed swimming and baseball. She knitted blankets for charity and made you a special one.

She had a sharp wit and wry humor. She was energetic and generous. I always enjoyed visiting with her and I count myself lucky for knowing her; she was a boisterous version of my own grandmother on my father's side who I loved. Nan passed away when you were very little and I don't expect you'll remember much of her but we have pictures for you and your mother has stories, as does your grandfather.

Frank Anthony Milletics

I never met your mother's grandfather who passed away when your mother was an adolescent. She recalls that he was a hardworking man, a master cabinet maker and carpenter by trade who built his own house which still stands in Mechanicsburg. He also built a house for "Uncle Dave" before he became ill and passed away in 1991. Pappy tells me that he enjoyed fast pitch softball and bowling.

Carlita S. Milletics (maiden name Scheffel)

Your grandmother is still a very important part of your life today! She is often here in our home and she is an important part of our family, we would not live so comfortably or happily without her regular generosity, particularly in terms of time shared with you and your sister so your mother and I can get chores done or simply get a nap.

She was born and raised in Bedford, Indiana. She worked at a Coca-Cola bottling plant there and saved an impressive collection of coins from vending machines. She came to Pennsylvania when her father was transferred to the Mechanicsburg Navy Depot. She got a job at Capitol Blue Cross where she worked when I met her.

I don't know a lot about her likes and interests. I do know she volunteered at a rescue in downtown Harrisburg when I met your mother. She once was in a bowling league and likes live entertainment of the sort you might expect on stage at a fair, local theatre and dinner theatre. She travels with some friends to dine at far flung locations around the state and enjoys shopping for things to gift you kids. She makes me laugh sometimes with a joke here and there her favorite pastime is quite obviously her grandchildren.

Fred and Mary Scheffel

Your grandmother's parents returned to Indiana a long time before I ever arrived here. We traveled to Bedford to meet them twice. Your great grandfather Fred Jason Scheffel was a paratrooper in World War II. He was a stooped slight fellow when I met him. He is of gentle nature and kind heart. I wish I had had a chance to know him better. Mary Alice Baker Scheffel is a firm believer in strict order in the home where. While she worked outside the home at times, she was primarily a homemaker. We visited them twice for two or three days at a time. They both wish they could have spent more time with you kids.

That is where we're from. Your mother and her family are like many central PA Dutch families, with a probable Slavic origin. My family and I are from Pacific Rim, we're boat people. You can claim Chinese, Hawaiian, European, English (Scotch & Irish actually), French and Jewish ancestry. If you were to take into account my biological father… I can't be sure. If someone asks you tell them what you want, we're American mutts now unburdened by a cumbersome "minority" surname that would make you susceptible to routine questions about your ethnic origins, *use that to your advantage.*

If you want to know where we come from or how we fit into some box or label on a government form, it's not important. We're good people. If you want to know who you are, where we come from remember *we are what we do,* each of us. We are not defined by where we came from or what land our ancestors called home. We are resilient, bold, honorable, nurturing, self-sacrificing, loving, hard-working sailors, warriors, care-givers, scholars, and athletes; imperfect and divine people of a virtue that is the product of habit.

Chapter 2

My Favorite Things

"...When this war is over I shall confine myself entirely to writing and painting."

-Winston Churchill

    My favorite things are not *things* at all. Those things most dear and enjoyable that are at once familiar and freshly surprising are my children, my wife, my extended family (Aloiau and Milletics) and my few friends. These things make me who I am more than the trivial matters of favorite films, foods and music. Still, some of these things have had a role in my ongoing self-creation or re-creation (recreation, coincidence?) So some of these trivial things might merit exploration here and might serve to amuse if not to inform so for posterity they are explored here before we move on to more important matters.

    My favorite thing that does not fit any of the categories is what happens every day when I come home. You and your sister come running screaming "daddy, daddy!" and I get hugs and questions about what I did that day. Miranda runs when I try to give her a hug, thinking I'll chase her and you ask "how was work daddy?" six times. I answer you "work was waffles!" and you laugh then ask "how was traffic daddy?" and I say again "waffles!" then we laugh. Coming home to that everyday never gets old. Your mom is usually stirring a pot behind you waiting for you kids to run off giggling so we can have a moment. That's my favorite thing of all.

Places

I always love the quiet corner of a room to watch the world unfold. A park bench or books store café nook to share a tender moment with your mother or alone with a favorite book before I had met her. That's more of a favorite thing to do though than a specific place, any book store or park bench might do.

The tugboats my father captained are the all-time favorite places for me as a child. The company that operated them dissolved and the tugs are gone but if there was a way I could spend a day on one I'd jump at the chance. The *Huki* was my favorite one of these vessels. It was white and blue, had two stacks and was very powerful. I also liked the *Maka'ala* but she sunk and nearly took my dad with her. The tug boats were tied up at pier 21, and there was a bunk house there for the sailors.

That place, the bunk house or "boat house" reeked of stale ashtrays and beer cans, body odor and pomade the sailors used to keep their hair in place. The window air conditioner unit was always set to maximum so you thought more about shivering than the smell. Sesame Street was often on the TV hanging over the card table. Our home never had air conditioning or a reliable TV connection so that might have had something to do with my preference for this place.

The beach at Lanikai is a favorite place for me and many others also love this beach known as one of the world's best. It's one of the few spots I was able to share with your mother when I took her to Hawaii in 2006. I never spent a lot of time on this tiny hidden beach when I was young because it was not easy to park there and it is far from anywhere I usually ventured. It's nice to visit because it's secluded, quiet and the sea is calm - perfect for relaxing and wading. A word of caution; if you visit you must be aware of the moon state. Consult a tidal calendar, for ten days following a new moon, there are many small jelly fish or man-o-war's washed up on the sand and these can make for a painful surprise.

Sand Island Beach Park was a day use area on the far southern end of Honolulu harbor that offered grilling and fishing as well as space to ride our bikes. Our family would take a cooler out there and cook on a hibachi and eat and play all day or just between my dad's sailings from Honolulu harbor and the boat house ten minutes away. My dad taught me to fish there and tie a lure. My cousin Daniel who was my best friend as a child was frequently along for the ride. There isn't another park like that around here. It would probably not impress anyone who grew up near Hershey Park though.

Hershey Park is a place I enjoyed but haven't visited much recently. It's harder to enjoy roller coasters as I get older, or with toddlers. It was the first place your mother and I went on an actual date after our first clumsy, tenuous meetings.

And finally the sea is my favorite place. I don't enjoy sailing for extended time across it but anywhere I can see it, smell it and feel it seems more real somehow, more like home to me. I'm always a little happier near the sea.

Books

My all-time first favorite book is by a fellow named Joseph Heller. He was a pacifist distrustful of authority for good reason. The book is widely considered to be a watershed moment in pacifist and subversive literature *Catch-22* tells the odd story of a hapless Lebanese immigrant named *Yossarian* who is pressed into military service as a World War II bombardier navigator in a B-25 squadron assigned to a fictitious squadron on a fictitious Mediterranean island filled with crazy characters.

The story is tragic and uplifting, unpredictable, surprising and hilarious while being infuriating and frightening as it shines the light of stark sanity and truth into the dark corners of untruth, self-deception and insanity that are required for industrialized warfare and other questionable endeavors required to create wealth for our secretive order of evil oligarchs.

The book was very popular when it was published and made Heller a household name briefly. Fans proudly displayed "Yossarian lives" bumper stickers on their cars that might indicate a question about the protagonist's fate at the end of the book but you'll have to read it to know. *Catch-22* has come to mean an inescapable situation, conundrum or seemingly insurmountable bureaucratic nightmare. If you ever consider a career in government or the military *you must read this book first*.

A Bridge Too Far is another wonderfully cautionary tale that says at once "don't join" the Army and if you do check everything twice before you go *anywhere*. It includes many lessons useful for life too, not just military service. If you don't want to read the book there is a mediocre film by the same name some big name stars. The story is about a tragic planning blunder of overly optimistic and arrogant leaders who failed to take simple precautions. When extending yourself ask, am I reaching a bridge too far? It's always served me well.

Of the soldiers in the story, Colonel Frost is one of my favorite characters. He and the other soldiers on both sides acquit themselves well proving they are the best western civilization has had to offer even as their inept leaders tragically squander their courage in an impossible endeavor. As with so many war stories there is dark humor and uplifting testimonials to the human spirit worth enjoying even if it only deepens the tragedy of loss.

If (God forbid) you end up in the infantry, I recommend Hackworth's *Steel my Soldiers Hearts*, and his *Vietnam Primer*. Read your field manuals, they are crap technically but can give you some useful lists and organizational tools, some pointers and help you with basic foundational knowledge that can serve you well.

You'd be surprised how many of the leaders you'll meet haven't bothered to read the manuals.

ALWAYS READ THE MANUAL!

Most of the books I know well are about war, it's been a constant in my life. *Man's Search for Meaning*, about finding meaning isn't about war but is set against the Second World War, also a favorite book. *Give us this Day* might be the Christian priest's version of this, a wonderful book from the pacific theater of the same war. *Flight of Eagles* and *Cold Harbor* are favorite fiction works, also set against European wars. The only non-war book on this list is *Midnight in the Garden of Good and Evil*. Your mother introduced me to its salacious and voyeuristic tale that proved intriguing enough for us to plan the first leg of our honeymoon in the books setting, Savannah. Your mother and I discussed this book on the night we met and so it has a special place in our hearts and our story.

Music

I have enjoyed lots of different music genres across my life course. My all-time favorite musical group is Iron Maiden. They had a complex rich operatic quality and seemed to me to be ahead of their time. They're amazing live. Their best work in my opinion was done prior to the Seventh Son album; there are some good tracks on that album but nothing interesting after it.

In the 1980s I enjoyed Metallica too. *Call of Cthulu*, *Creeping Death* and *Damage Inc.* are probably my favorite pieces. In the 1990s I enjoyed Garbage; their front woman has a compelling timbre. Garbage recorded the best James Bond movie theme song ever (by far) and many other fun pieces that might be described as euro-pop-bubble gum but enjoyable nonetheless. In the 2000s I discovered System of a Down and their violent, wrathful anxiety. They pound out manic, profane and stirring hymnals of war and freedom against oppression and commercialism.

Some notables: I enjoy new age music at my desk at the office, Gregorian chant or Enya for instance. I used to listen to Enya's *Watermark* in Bosnia every day to help me sleep. Some classical music is also very enjoyable for me. I particularly like Bach; his solo cello suites are my favorite works for background music at work or driving and the cello is my favorite instrument. I also enjoy Beethoven. I took your mom to the Baltimore symphony once to hear his 9th with another couple. I once enjoyed Wagner but I no longer care for him. I enjoy a wide array of classical music, but I'm no expert.

Vacations

If I could magically teleport anywhere in the world to relax for a week (or three) it would be Hawaii. But it's fourteen hours away and costs a fortune to get to. So these days my favorite vacation spot is the coast of Virginia where I feel safe and comfortable taking you and your mother. Cape Henry has a small military resort that's one of the better kept secrets of the service. It's nostalgic for me as I was stationed in the area during my first Navy tour and I enjoy catching a glimpse of my old ship from the bay bridge as we arrive there. That the ship is due to retire this year is not a fact lost one me; it's been a cause for some reflection.

Your mother and I spent part of our honeymoon at Cape Henry. We started in Savannah and stopped in Charleston on our way to Cape Henry where we spent only a night or two. When we pulled into Charleston we got roped into a time share sales pitch to get a free overnight stay. Before going to the pitch we stopped for lunch at the local Irish Pub. Everywhere your mother and I go together the Irish Pub is one of the first places we seek out. We judge the entire city by the first impression the pub makes. Irish Pubs (anywhere) are favorite places. Our hometown has a terrific authentic Irish Pub "Gary Owens" with great food, live music a lively atmosphere and friendly staff, it's a true gem.

I've spent time touring the world and I think that Palma de Mallorca, Rhodes and other Greek spots in the Mediterranean are also wonderful places I've enjoyed but I don't think I can relax there as much as I can at Cape Henry, Savannah or Hawaii.

Film

I love film, bad films, good films, independent films, horror films, zombies, giant monsters from outer space even lousy made for TV films on the SyFy channel that usually feature a giant shark or octo-gator which eats a town full of bad actors who die searching for a plot. My all-time favorite films might depend on the mood I'm in. Sometimes I want to watch a rousing adventure or story about friendship or monsters or friends *and* monsters, why not?

But because I have such diverse tastes in film my favorite film is a "chick flick". *The Princess Bride* has it all; swordfights, war, murder, torture, intrigue, giants, monsters, a princess, pirates, true-love and miracles. What's not to love? *The Painted Veil* is another "chick flick" (and independent foreign film) that I enjoyed with your mother. It's dreadful in pace and terribly tragic but features terrific performances by all the primary players and a breathtaking setting. Good film, not in my top ten but deserving an honorable mention. *The Sand Pebbles* is a niche film for Steve McQueen fans and Navy men that is a favorite. It runs the length of a baseball game so clear your schedule if you are going to attempt to watch it.

I also love *Jaws*, a great manly flick. Men vs. supernatural monster – and yes the shark is somewhat supernatural in the flick but just subtly so. Three men representing different masculine archetypes join forces to destroy a dangerous predator. It's based on a Peter Benchley novel, one of its taglines hints at the shark being the devil's creation[4].

Well there are a lot of great films out there to enjoy. Learning to enjoy even terrible films is a skill of sorts I'm happy to have developed for when the weather is rotten outside. Just a brief list of favorites: *Empire Strikes Back, The Wrath of Khan, The Outlaw Josey Wales, Pale Rider, Unforgiven, Midway, Monty Python and Holy Grail* to name just a few favorites that are easier to find on the internet than *The Sand Peebles*.

Food

I love to cook. It's an important skill for a young man to obtain if not master. I enjoy using fresh herbs and produce from our own garden and fresh experiments in the kitchen that fuse your mother's and my own distinct culinary styles. Your mother and I especially enjoy having time to cook together. We like to relax and take too much time to pick out some ingredients and spend an afternoon putting something complex together on a lazy no football Sunday.

---

[4] The paperback copy I had said something like "it's as if god gave evil a body and the devil gave it …Jaws" i wish i still had that.

I love summer foods the most; things I can grill and winter foods second, thick or hearty soups and udon noodles (good anytime). A short list of favorite individual food items include: *Musubi, Malasadas, Manapua, Kal-bi short ribs, Poi, Kalua Pork and Lamb chops*. And let's not forget wine, liquid poetry it is, and there is nothing more civilized.

That is pretty much it, a collection of my favorite things. Not everything made this list. Some are infrequently enjoyed things or so obscure or similar to another thing on the list there is no point in mentioning them. These things that made the list I've enjoyed and never tire of, some are influential and have had a formative effect on me. The books are full of important ideas and there is no doubt *Catch-22* shaped my mildly subversive perspective. Film too can be quite influential, I found in film role models which my life was sadly lacking.

An example of a fictitious film character as role model is Captain Kirk. He was a source of leadership role modeling having once said something like "never ask one of your men to do something you aren't willing to do yourself." Thankfully, there are other less fictitious people who have had an even greater influence. These people could rightfully be called "Heroes" and so I will explore that important subject next.

Chapter 3

Heroes

"He has all of the virtues I dislike and none of the vices I admire."

-Winston Churchill

Heroes come in many shapes and sizes. None of them are perfect but to some significant, wondrous and exciting extent exemplify something we wish to find in ourselves. My father for example, while prone to completely inappropriate violence was a heroic if not epic example of honor and a tremendous work ethic. Literary and real characters are imperfect, we all are; perfection is un-relatable and thus unsuitable for a hero. Seeking perfection in others and yourself will lead only to disappointment.

This book is in part the result of a successful search for my own masculinity and finding validation of my being, not from my father, mother or anyone else but by my own reckoning. It's been a difficult search, the loss of my father temporarily plunged me into a depression in part founded on the notion that I might never receive validation from him. I was worried he would never see in me the achievements that would finally make me complete and successful in his eyes; while he was alive I often disappointed him. He is my first hero and for several reasons.

First he was my dad, he didn't have to be but he chose to be. It wasn't easy to be sure but he made an honest effort. My own father and at least one other would be father had turned away from me and my mother but not Frank. He could have settled for being a step parent but instead opted to adopt me to give me the gift of a true father, the same name as my siblings and Hawaiian-Chinese heritage.

Michael Chandler

This makes my parents decision to inform me of the adoption somewhat perplexing. I suppose I would have guessed it based on the fact that I looked like a Mexican or Indian kid while my father and his relatives were all Chinese and my sisters were also more classically Asian in appearance. The only thing I can think of is that he sought to impress upon me how much he loved me and that's the reason I chose to attribute to that decision to adopt me and reveal it.

As I had said before my father was a man of salt and iron, and his word was his bond. If he said something he followed through no matter the cost or obstacle. When the weather was hard and others called off sick, or around the holidays when there was an emergency and no one else would answer the phone to come in and handle an emergency my father would always respond.

He would go, and he'd make a few calls himself and chide the lollygaggers and malingers into coming to work. The other sailors were more afraid of what my father thought of them than of their employer, their management or the union. They knew that disappointing my father would be a black mark their reputations might not easily recover from since so many others came to him for counsel when promotions were being considered.

My dad's history was inspiring to me as well. He served in the Army during World War II, which is a war unlike any of our modern wars that I have known. Today we go to war almost casually, less than 1% of our people participate and we have nothing like our survival at stake. And in World War II nothing less than our countries existence was in jeopardy.

My father being a Hawaiian took the Japanese attack on Pearl Harbor quite personally. He served in the Army, where you could reasonably expect to be wounded or killed[5]. The entire country mobilized, all of industry the media – all of the country was at war. His service in uniform influenced my decision to enlist in the Navy and to later seek a tour with the Army.

I realized when writing this book that I have surpassed my father's military achievements in terms of rank attained and time in service, including time under threat of hostile fire and in close proximity to something that could be called an enemy. This is luck of the draw only though and not an achievement in itself. Hopefully there is never anything like World War II again.

---

[5] Over 2% of Earth's population died as a result of the Second World War. Over 400,000 U.S. persons were wounded or killed.

That war provides a number of heroes. Winston Churchill and General Patton were both epic figures before this war but often most renowned for what they contributed to the world in that conflict. They were both very wealthy men who had every advantage growing up, they didn't face anything like the hardships Lo Yau Wong did coming to Hawaii in 1865 but they struck a chord with me for a number of other reasons.

Winston Churchill was in addition to being a statesman and terrific orator was a soldier, like my father except that he served as a commissioned officer. He was a prisoner of war in the Boer War who had managed to escape and return to the fight. He won a Nobel Prize for literature and was an avid painter. He had a work ethic like my father's. Churchill was known to be up and working at two in the morning and drove his staff mad with early hour summons to critical meetings at his office where he would be in his pajamas enjoying soup while considering some question of strategy.

He was also notable for his steadfast loyalty not only to his country which had at one point rejected him, but his fidelity to his wife. He was an odd fellow who did not present the typical appearance of a warrior you might expect. He was stout and round, with thick jowls. He possessed an acerbic humor stemming perhaps from his fondness of liquor combined with his towering intellect. Churchill read as many as five books at a time saying "you're only as good as the last book you read."

General George Patton was overly aggressive but this was part of his success, what made him so effective and noteworthy. He didn't shrink from holding people accountable for their results. He didn't focus on actions and praise folks for unproductive action or smarts (as many do) but recognized only results.

He was also a spiritual anomaly, believing himself to be a reincarnated soldier, an old soul who had been in many wars on many battlefields before throughout time. He kept a bible at his bedside and read it daily, but his belief in reincarnation was not strictly in keeping with his Christian education. He wrote poetry and read extensively. He was bombastic and irreverent but he was a *genius for war*. [6]

As a young man I felt that history pointed towards more war in the future. I looked to leaders like him for insights into war that might provide a key to survival on some far away continent where I inevitably would find myself one day. That was a horrible thing for a young person to worry about,

---

[6] This was the subtitle of a highly recommended book about Patton actually. I prefer *War as I Knew It*.

I don't wish for you to have to worry about such things. Churchill and Patton provided a lot of good ideas for me as a young man. Later as a professional soldier I looked to the writings of Colonel David Hackworth and Colonel John Boyd for more technical and timely knowledge, though it is also beneficial to revisit Churchill for a laugh and new insights missed in previous readings.

Colonel Hackworth or "Hack" taught the basics. Take care of your men, trust them. On plans he said keep it sledge hammer simple (KISS). He didn't seek glory as Patton did (one of Patton's shortcomings) or political office; in fact he left the Army disgraced never again to hold public office for acting boldly on a matter of conscience. Colonel Boyd was the creator of Energy=Maneuver Theory (or EM Theory) and father of the modern fighter weapons (Top Gun) school. He was a modern samurai sword fighter[7] who gave us a great decision making and opponent analyzing tool the OODA "loop". Col. Boyd also challenged his followers to "Do Something" for this country rather than "Be Somebody" for themselves. He chose to do something important, which kept him from becoming a General, which he wanted to be but not at the cost of his conscience.

All of these men are men of conscience, all are warriors and all suffered setbacks and sacrificed much for their loved ones, communities and countries. They earned their place in history the hard way. Hack was critically wounded three times (all head wounds) and died of cancer resulting from his service in Vietnam. I have an autographed copy of his *Vietnam Primer*, it is a prized possession.

Col Boyd had his career ended prematurely and others have taken credit for his accomplishments and still others have worked to erase his influence and achievements. Incidentally Col Boyd is from Pennsylvania, Erie to be exact where he was a lifeguard in his youth.

Churchill was driven from office once and had few if any friends worth mentioning. Revisionists focus on his racist tendencies, evident they argue in his dealings with colonial holdings in Guiana and Haiti, but his perspective on race is not outside the norm of the milieu in which he lived.

Patton died in Europe at the conclusion of his campaign. He was never able to return home to see his beloved wife. He suffered public disgrace

---

[7] In the tradition of Miyamoto Musashi, see *The Book of the Five Rings*

for a terrible decision[8] and was denied key honors and victories he desired including the chance to take Berlin, an "honor" given to the Russians.

My father never finished high school and never had anything nice or new for himself. With one exception, when after years of fighting for a disability settlement with his employer, my dad set aside a small piece of that to buy a new motorcycle to replace his 1973 sportster. In 1986 he sold that bike for $3,000, more than double its original purchase price in 1973 of $1,300.

Reaching further back in time we find some of the fathers of this stoic ethic of service to something larger than the self, to community or country. Marcus Aurelius is a favorite amongst these. He was a Roman emperor[9] whose writings have been central to my own outlook.

Our Chinese ancestors have important personalities too. Sun Tzu is one; however he may be a fictitious character – a composite of several great generals. There are Confucius and Lao Tzu as well, both fathers of large and influential belief systems. We're not actually related to any of them but we they are a part of our heritage. Between the two I prefer Lao Tzu over Confucius. Sun Tzu is probably the most influential of the three with respect to my life. He (if indeed he existed) wrote the *Art of War*.

That book is not only a flawless path to victory to those who would wisely consider and apply its principles, it is a genuine piece of literary art and tool for improved self-awareness. In a word the *Art of War* is deception. But it is not that easy. You'll have to read it and spend much time contemplating its meaning as many masters have if you wish to know the path to ultimate victory. I can't teach it to you; he can't teach it to you. Follow the guide, study, contemplate and you will find the way if you seek it.

All of these men are warriors and statesmen, but I do not agree with Patton who said that "next to war all other human endeavors shrink to insignificance." War is an aberration, an unfortunate dark side of our freedom and a dangerous extension of our appetites in excess. There are many more worthwhile endeavors, indeed nearly any endeavor is more praise worthy. It is an unfortunate part of my own life that I was equipped for little else.

---

[8] Patton famously assaulted an enlisted man in hospital for "cowardice". Regardless of the man's medical condition or lack thereof you cannot assault a subordinate. Patton may one day be most remembered for this lapse.
[9] From 161 to 180 A.D., the last of the "Five Good Emperors"

This is not to say I lacked an interest in other things, or heroes who were not warriors. Jacques-Yves Cousteau (1910-1997) was a famous marine explorer who gave the world advanced scuba technology and conducted ground breaking research on his floating laboratory the *Calypso*. He and his crews adventures were the subject of my all-time favorite TV show the *Undersea World of Jacque Cousteau*. He wrote many books too and established a society for marine conservation to which I briefly belonged.

While Jacques-Yves Cousteau was an officer in the WWII French Navy's "information service" (a kind of Special Forces or spy group) this is not what he is most know for and I never knew anything about that part of his life until I fact checked his dates of birth and death while writing this paragraph. His post war life is what matters to me, his scientific work, his conservation efforts and his love of the sea.

I wanted to live at sea like he did in peace but I didn't have the chance. My parents were unprepared to even begin to point me towards a foundation that might help me pull myself up to that level of achievement or to enter that field (math & chemistry). There was one brief moment when I thought there might be a way but it faded quickly. Charitably I choose to assume they knew I'd find my own way to whatever was best for me believing the universe will unfold as it should.

History is replete with great men (and women) who accomplished a great many laudable feats. Undoubtedly you'll find some of your own heroes. That's part of the fun of life finding a bit of yourself in heroes and inversely a bit of them in yourself. I can only hope to be counted amongst them one day. You might find that like friends you outgrow some heroes or abandon them all together as you grow in confidence and character on your own, but it's always nice to have a friend or two you can count on or a hero to encourage us with their shining example. Now we will begin to look at a core value my heroes have exemplified, the importance of learning and knowledge.

Chapter 4

The Importance of Learning

"Never regard something as doing you good if it makes you betray a trust or lose your sense of shame or makes you show hatred, suspicion, ill-will or hypocrisy or a desire for things best done behind closed doors."

-Marcus Aurelius, Roman Emperor

I never dared to image that one day I would be sitting here writing about how important it is to learn everything you can about whatever interests you. I didn't always value learning. I had mistaken my father's lack of a high school education and my mother's attainment of a mere high school diploma to as a license to ignore school.

I flunked the seventh grade. The next year I was put in an expensive Junior Achievement program which put me in courses at the college level and let me make up 7th grade while completing 8th grade at the same time[10]. That made school seem that much less relevant. I came to believe that education didn't matter. I failed to connect our family's frequent hardships with their lack of education. They certainly failed to properly communicate that but not for lack of trying.

I then failed to complete high school, causing me to steer an atypical life course. I found my way to college eventually thanks to the help of good friends, caring strangers, luck and my service to my country which provided funds for study of all sorts. But I never attended a graduation ceremony.

---

[10] I aced all my classes except *Math* &*French* finishing with a B & D respectively.

Michael Chandler

Like Moses who could not enter the Promised Land, I will never cross the stage to receive a diploma. A karmic debt I earned for having wasted so many opportunities. I will be looking forward to your college graduations and drive you relentlessly to get there so I can attend a graduation ceremony. No pressure or anything, just do your best. College is important, but there are other important ways of learning too.

Experience is the best teacher of course, but it can be costly and cruel (or lethal). Academic settings are important for foundational knowledge in preparation for experience. This can save your skin, so read the manuals. There are many different kinds of knowledge and different ways to attain or even define it. The question of "what is knowledge?" is central to the field I chose for graduate studies. While fascinating to me, it's not worth exploring in detail here.

What is important to impart to you going forward is that wherever you are or whatever you're doing consider what you might be able to learn while you're there. There is almost nothing that isn't worth learning if the opportunity presents itself. There are many seemingly trivial or burdensome activities that we can benefit from in terms of learning and growing though we might not perceive a value or purpose for the knowledge at the time. We never know what the invisible unknowable might have in store for us!

To be certain I didn't always think this way, particularly in my youth when all too often I was busy thinking about what I'd rather be doing, where I would rather be or how best to get away from whatever awful situation I was in. I was often distracted, struck with wanderlust and sometimes depressed or desperate to just escape. Sometimes I was just hungry. But I learned from this too.

My parents showed how career and education choices can limit freedom and harm security. I am a happier adult now knowing how hard it was when I was a child. I am able to appreciate the smallest things and find wonder and beauty in unexpected places. I am better equipped to prepare you and your siblings to prepare for learning and attempting to attain your dreams than my parents were, thanks to them. I have less excuse if I fail you.

Your grandfather thought learning was very important. He had very limited academic learning which was interrupted by World War II. He witnessed the attack on Oahu by the Imperial Japanese Navy on December 7th, 1941. My father tried as best he could to pass along lessons I was not always ready to learn. He would give me seemingly endless lectures and quizzes on world geography, his favorite topic (Geography is about the future). Even someone without a fancy education can teach us much.

The Ox and Scorpio

Dad encouraged me to read extensively and tried to get me to participate in completing crossword puzzles with him but more often than not I wouldn't sit still to entertain his frustrating lessons often utilizing the Sunday New York Times puzzle, known to be of the highest difficulty. I do remember from time to time knowing an answer or two and being very impressed with myself.

I know if my dad had a better academic background, he'd have been able to better articulate his beliefs about the importance of learning and he would have been better equipped to guide me and my sisters towards academic and career goals. Thankfully, I later came to realize the importance of academic learning – and its role in life learning. In part, that is the purpose of this small collection of short stories, warnings, refrains and encouragements, to help you be ready to accept and appreciate opportunities my father and I had missed.

Learning is a core value for our family. It's a part of who we are. Our great ancestor Lo Yao Wong valued education and learning so much he built a school for his village (and other things too). Your Pappy sacrificed his future to help your mother get a formal education. My mother made it a priority to finish high school despite having a new born to care for. My own father despite his lack of academic training was always trying to teach, with a hands-on approach.

Everything was a learning opportunity for him, a day on the boat meant a chance to learn how to tie a dozen knots (I mastered only a handful), a night sailing? Let's learn some star names and how to find them during different times of the year without a telescope (we couldn't afford one). It was constant with him. A day at the restaurant cleaning the place was an opportunity to demonstrate how to see to the customer's needs, how to treat the customers and care for the business. He didn't always communicate well nor have the patience to deal with a small child but he sure did try and he had some success.

I learned unusual things from my father. I learned the capitol of every country on earth, the names of over a hundred important navigation stars, how to find Polaris and lifesaving rope and knife tricks. I learned to respect the sea and love all peoples no matter their race or origin. Because I see the the world from the sea, I understand the transient nature in all things. I see every urgent concern of man as only a moment that will ebb with the tide. I fear little because I rarely knew stability, safety or security. I had to be ready to deal with anything with swift calm resolve. I know that honor has no price and cannot be easily mended. Money means freedom not happiness. He taught me that a man lets his actions speak for him and words are worth little.

I know nothing is more expensive than regret. He taught me life is full of surprises and that we must adapt in part because he had trouble doing this.

This is the greatest of skills, the ability to adapt quickly and appropriately. In the *Tao-Te Ching* [11] you find the most important survival words I have heard "be like water". Faced with a difficult situation, adapt. Let go of the prison of form or dogma and deal with the situation before you as it demands to be dealt with. When dropped into a glass, be like water which takes the shape of the glass and is unharmed. Be ever as water. Strong and supple, the sea topples mountains; water gives life and can take it. The *Scorpio* is a water sign, be like water is my motto, the way.

There are a great many things I learned from my father, my family and my upbringing, far too many to attempt to capture here. These are but a few highlights as Act I is intended for a young man preparing but not yet out on his own. There are more lessons we'll touch on later. For a young man, there is only one thing more important than learning and adaptability and my father taught me that too. Manners and how you treat people. This and this alone is the most important thing for a young man to learn and to know.

---

[11] a canonical work of sorts for Taoists.

Chapter 5

Manners

"When you wake up in the morning, tell yourself: The people I deal with today will be meddling, ungrateful, arrogant, dishonest, jealous, and surly. They are like this because they can't tell good from evil. But I have seen the beauty of good, and the ugliness of evil, and have recognized that the wrongdoer has a nature related to my own—not of the same blood or birth, but the same mind, and possessing a share of the divine."

-Marcus Aurelius

Consideration for others, their feelings and exceeding expectations with a cheerful, courteous demeanor (as appropriate to the circumstance) will always convey a sense of sincerity, caring and class that will reflect upon you and your family for years to come. You want to impress someone as a young man, show up fifteen minutes early, for everything, every time[12]. You want someone to listen to you so you can impress them with what you know? Smile and listen to what they have to say first, pause. Let it soak in. Include what they said; reference it in whatever you say. Share your thoughts, don't drive points. I know you're smart, you know you're smart and heck you might be but it doesn't matter if you're rude even if you're right. Courtesy opens ears, minds and doors. Disrespect perceived because of discourtesy has started wars.

Act with integrity, it's extremely discourteous to be insincere. Don't make promises; make commitments and keep them. If appropriate, don't

---

[12] Sometimes called the *Lombardi Rule*, I call it being on *Sergeant Time* as I adopted this practice as a Noncommissioned Officer.

bother talking, just do it. Let your actions speak for you. They speak louder and with more authority than any awkward teenager (and most adults) can. When dealing with adults remember they're busy and have little time to pay attention to anything a young person might say. This is doubly true if that young person is rude or brusque. Show up, shut up, smile and listen. That's all you got to do right now. That and your homework, chores and pick a college.

Picking a college is something we'll talk about another time. Manners are infinitely more important than your institutional choice. Manners are a little thing, small and easy to do if sometimes tough to remember. I hope this section is something you feel comfortable skipping. Your mother and I have tried to impress upon you early that *everybody likes a polite child*. It's no accident that some of your first words were "please" and "thank you". Some of your first multi-world sentences were "drink please" or "cookie please" and "thank you mommy". Maybe we only succeeded in teaching how awesome cookies are, so this section will serve to help you reflect on the true lessons begun in your first eighteen months when you were already saying please with little or no prompting.

One reason this will be so valuable to you is that manners and common courtesy are simply fading away in our increasingly hasty and coarsening world. As you become an adult, habits formed early will become second nature – automatic and a part of your character. By acting polite, with concern for others, we become polite and properly concerned with others. It will help you stand out as an island of civility in a sea of rude self-absorbed barbarians.

You might see others not being polite, taking or getting things despite being rude, it's the way of things. Don't let it get you down. Nice guys don't always get the girl or whatever but in the long run you'll fare better and virtue is its own reward. Those other guys - see where they are in 20 years. The jerks I knew growing up are still doing the same minimum wage slave jobs they had in high school, or in prison. Some are struggling to support two kids and paying alimony to their ex-wife, their one time high school sweetheart. The guys who got the big money Wall Street jobs are pan handling now or in the unemployment line in the deep economic downturn our country is in at the time of this writing, 20 years after they left high school in 1992.

When confronted rudely, pause. Do not let an adversary control you and raise your ire. Do not *react*. Do not act out of anger. The better part of valor is discretion[13]. It's better to give some ground, even apologize and try to

---

[13] As a favorite Shakespearian character *Falstaff* famously quipped.

understand a rude or irate person. You're my son you'll know how to stop a person with your hands, but mauling or embarrassing someone is not going to impress anyone, earn you any friends or make anyone think better of you when words or a polite concession would have diffused a situation. For restraint of your strength you will cultivate an image of Valor and grow Honor. With one exception, which is an important reason we don't live in the kind of neighborhood I grew up in.

We don't allow bullies to victimize our family or prey on the weak. Kids used to pick on my sisters growing up. They would injure them for amusement. Boys mostly, would bully them for whatever reason. I took a lot of lumps dispensing justice and defending my sisters from violent idiots without the upbringing to know enough to treat others. We are men of peace because we choose to be meek.[14] I complain about my father's violence because it was sometimes directed at me and my sisters or my mother. But I've also seen him forced into a situation where he had defend his family.

I went a bit overboard on occasion when defending my sisters. I lost a friend once when he pushed my sister down hard. I hit him so hard he collapsed, vomited and lost control of his bladder. I regret that. Hurting someone, striking them or embarrassing them with hard words or rudeness isn't something you can take back. Once it's done, it's done and can be costly to *you*. In an argument even if you're right, it doesn't matter if you're rude. If you fight, don't do more harm than you need to.

Now I want to wrap up what is intended to be the smallest chapter of this book. This should be old hat to you and serve only as a reminder should you feel you have lost your way or wonder what you might one day want to teach your sons should I be lost to an unfortunate accident. Be polite. Listen, be early, gentle, sincere, and true to your word no matter the cost.

We are as we do.

---

[14] In the original Greek, 'strength restrained' by self-discipline and wisdom 'weak' 'helpless' or 'incapable'.

ACT I Curtain

"Not to feel exasperated or defeated or despondent because your days aren't packed with wise and moral actions. But to get back up when you fail, to celebrate behaving like a human—however imperfectly—and fully embrace the pursuit you've embarked on."

-Marcus Aurelius

Born to an unwed teen mother with nothing, having to endure abandonment by my father and a second temporary father[15] then developing learning disabilities due to a near death experience[16], I faced a stacked deck from the start. I struggled to understand how I fit into the world and with answering who I was in the face of skepticism from everyone I encountered who would judge me by my answer to their question about my race. I had no clear expectations to meet or map and so I drifted. I watched family and friends die before I had even set out on my own. I excelled at nothing, I mastered nothing. I plodded and trudged on as an *Ox*, yoked to a load impossible to pull towards an unclear horizon across a desert full of hungry, hateful aliens.

Sometimes there was shelter in my family home, quiet and even good times but when I should have been preparing to go to off to college or to begin a career I was lost without focus. I collected social security disability for a while when what I was told was epilepsy, that plagued me most of my youth, flared up in my late teens. I was unfit for sailing or any of the jobs a high school dropout could qualify for. With poor financial resources and a

---

[15] My mother was married to Joseph Francese for less than 1 year.
[16] The drowning at Pier 21 left me with a speech impediment, epilepsy, dyslexia and what might be termed ADHD.

social network that had gone on ahead without me, I struggled to make it alone.

Yes I played guitar in what you might call a band, but we were so awful we were never going to pay the bills with our music. My band mates met girls and had kids before they were twenty. One joined the Army at 17 or 19. My sisters needed help too; they were still in school and struggling. I was of little help to them. For a time we were all split up too as my parents feuding drove my mother to relocate to the mainland briefly, Nika joined her for a while. I stayed with friends to avoid my father who was particularly volatile during this time and Didi joined me for part of this period as well. She had the least trouble getting along with dad so she didn't completely move out at this time.

I don't tell you this to make excuses for my poor decisions or mistakes in my early life. I want to paint a picture, if a dizzying one of what things were like for me as I prepared to set out on my own and what my state of mind was. Essentially I was lost and adrift. Then I decided to set my own course. It took a while because as an *Ox*, I usually make decisions and change directions slowly and cautiously in my own time. I had a lot of learning of various sorts as I discussed but I had no idea what was useful and what wasn't, how to tie it all together and use it. Fear and confusion was being replaced by shame and finally some ambition.

So I looked to heroes and my father who is first amongst them. I wanted to make him proud, to do right by him as I said in the introduction to achieve some validation. I knew from literature that a hero's tale begins with a *departure* or *call to adventure*[17]. Captain Kirk left Iowa for deep space, Moses was exiled from Egypt and our great ancestor Lo Yau Wong had gone amongst the foreigners across the sea to seek his fortune. So I had a star to steer by finally given to me by literature, art and the legends of great men including my father and great ancestor.

I went across the sea into a foreign land to seek my fortune amongst a strange people. I left Hawai'i for "the mainland"[18] to work amongst the *Haoles*[19] with their strange language[20] and ways. Like my ancestor I went with nothing more than I could carry in a suitcase or bag. It was February 1995, I

---

[17] See Joseph Campbell's *The Hero with a Thousand Faces* for detail of heroes across time and an explanation of this books organization.
[18] What Hawaiians call the 48 contiguous states of the United States of America
[19] White person; any foreigner.
[20] English in Hawaii is as different from North American English it is from British English.

flew into Chicago's O'Hare Airport and the temperature was in the teens with a wind chill below zero. I was wearing a worn tank top, shorts and rubber beach comber sandals. When I left the airport terminal for the bus and felt a bitter cold I had never encountered before I wondered "what have I got myself into?"

ACT II
INITIATION

Michael Chandler

Chapter 6

Career

"A man does what he must - in spite of personal consequences, in spite of obstacles and dangers and pressures - and that is the basis of all human morality."

-Winston Churchill

When you are little, people will ask you "what do you want to be when you grow up?" and they mean to ask "what job would you like to do or expect to do?" I struggled with this because I wanted to work as an X, Y, or Z but generally didn't know how to achieve a career as an X, Y or Z. I didn't believe I had the capability to be an L, M, N Or P either, let alone an X. Jacques-Yves Cousteau's exploits inspired me to try and be a Marine Biologist. I was in the right place; Hawai'i has some of the best resources to launch a career in this field. Unfortunately I lacked the basic academic prerequisites, funds and a number of other things that are required to pursue this career.

I wanted to be a writer but it can take a lifetime to achieve even modest success, a significant gamble and one of the first rules is to write what you know. Chefs write cook books, generals write about leadership and war, scientists write about physics and doctors write about drugs. It seemed that I had to figure out what I would be when I grew up before I could be a writer.

I tried music for which you just need a peaceful place to practice. This was something my family could not provide, so my musical skills didn't develop.

With my frail constitution professional athlete wasn't a career option, so what would I be when I grew up? I have only recently found that answer. Along the way I've had a dozen careers and lived a life of swashbuckling high adventure- living, loving and suffering as much as any dozen other people.

The suffering part is why I would not recommend my approach to finding a career.

Picking a career can be tough, if you don't already have something in mind by the time you're nearing high school graduation then you should stop whatever it is you're doing *right now* and begin exploring some options. You don't have to know right away. Know that every career has ups and downs, benefits and costs - find the combination that fits you. After telling you about the path I took I'll discuss briefly some things I know about other careers I considered or didn't and why.

A First Step

The Navy had seemed a logical choice for a career. I had lived in a magical land which was free because it was protected by the Navy, no Navy- no Hawaii. The Navy is an enormous job provider and pumps tens of millions in the economy each year. Movies like *Midway* and elementary school field trips to the USS Arizona Memorial made it clear how pivotal our Navy was to American and world history. Captain Kirk was a *ship captain*, not an astronaut. Jacques-Yves Cousteau lived on the sea, my father had spent most of his career as a sailor and he had spent time in the Navy reserve. Many of the best sailors with his company were former Navy sailors or Coast Guardsmen. I couldn't afford the merchant marine academy or even the community college version available in Seattle and the Coast Guard recruiter never returned my calls, so I enlisted into the Navy.

The Navy and I have had a very rocky relationship. To begin with I had requested enlistment as a Quartermaster (QM) and had signed a contract guaranteeing that "rating" but weeks after signing the contract, on the day of departure the Navy decided it wanted me to be an Operations Specialist (OS) instead. I reluctantly agreed to switch to OS because I had already cut all my ties to home. I couldn't stop the momentum and had to go along with the Navy's request. I can guess that making a stand on that hill would have ended badly.

I did well in "Boot Camp" finishing first academically, earning a letter of commendation from the school house commander and an award from the Sons of the American Revolution, Illinois Chapter. I was one of a handful of

The Ox and Scorpio

new recruits who had won an award for various feats. We were taken aside after the large graduation ceremony to a special reception with an admiral and a local congressman. I remember there was an enormous cake and it was quite bland. My father wanted to attend but couldn't his mother had passed away. I left boot camp that night, a few days before my classmates would depart so that I might attend her funeral. I was asked to eulogize my grandmother, before all others in full dress uniform standing before a crowd of what seemed like a thousand people, before a wall length portrait of her in a World War I navy blue nurses' uniform.

I flew directly to Virginia from Hawaii to radar school and decided the OS rating wasn't for me after I was given orders to the USS Ponce. The ship has a long unremarkable career as a Marine transport but she was a garbage scow in my eyes. A fat, slow, ugly barge. She was not a ship of the line, somehow I had it in my mind she was not worthy. So I managed to be sent out to the fleet as a Boatswain's Mate (BM) which would be roughly equivalent to a Quartermaster for merchant marine licensing after I left the Navy.

I had some rough detours along the way but I found my way to the USS Enterprise, a right proper ship of the line, a flagship – one in which an Admiral would embark. Enterprise has a long, proud history and a mythic quality thanks in part to her popular culture fame. I got my first glimpse of her from fifteen thousand feet through the side window or a tiny cargo plane on approach to the ship. After the shuddering landing I stepped out onto the cacophonous flight deck and thought "this is where I belong!"

When I landed on the "Big-E" she was preparing for a six month cruise which became seven after a short detour near the end. I would qualify as a lee helmsman and coxswain, teaching others how to do what I grew up doing on my dad's lap - driving boats (though Enterprise was a good deal larger). I drove the Enterprise through the Suez Canal which was quite difficult and pulled some other tough duties. Out of respect for the dead I won't write in detail about that cruise. More than a dozen souls were lost, the Navy won't confirm the actual number who died during this trip but an average carrier deployment sees at least four and an average of six fatalities during the 90s when I sailed aboard Enterprise. It was the hardest thing I've ever done in my life. I've never worked harder. I've never been so near to death so many times. I never before glimpsed the benevolent divine. It was a life changing seven months.

After the cruise, an interminable dry dock period found me on the mess decks refilling ketchup bottles. There was little work for a boat driver in a dry dock. My family could use my help at home and so I went home. Of course you can never really go home. My father's health was failing and it was nice to see him smile when I arrived. He was genuinely happy to see me, he was proud of me.

I obtained a merchant mariners license, referred to as Z-card and tried sailing professionally using my dad's union contacts to get some good sailings quickly jumping ahead of hundreds of other underemployed sailors on the waiting list. I had to respond to short notice calls for week long trips or accept hazardous sailings but I could make more than $4,000 a month if I stayed afloat. That was the real trick, a lot of the old timers and regulars called off after seeing a weather report threatening heavy seas during the winter, I sailed most regularly from November 1997 to February 1998. By the time March had come, there were no more sailings, no more bad weather reports to scare the old timers off and so I had to find another career.

Something else had happened to me too. I wanted to settle down. I had lived the great adventure and had acquired some new skills and discovered my strength (or so I thought). Now I wanted to use that to establish myself and maybe start a family of my own. I realized that I didn't want to put my sons through what my father had put me through. I felt like an orphan when he had longer sailings, taking him away for weeks or months at a time. I had to find a land based skill-set to be a proper father.

Leaving the sea was a step back. My time in the Navy hadn't given me any land based non-weapons related skills. But it did give me great confidence I had lacked before and a firm belief everything I did after the Navy would be easy. Without college, I could only take odd jobs and focus on helping my mother and father. My father became bed ridden and once my mother got him into a stable situation with in home nursing aides, I had to set out on my own again. I wasn't able to carry my own weight and even if I was able to help with my father's medical care my family couldn't afford to feed me. I travelled to Washington State to seek work like so many Hawaiian's had done in recent years. That was almost a disaster.

My travelling companion funded the trip and determined Moses Lake was the place to go. It's in east central Washington. We ended up stopping for an overnight rest in Ellensburg and stayed there for a while. The town was a quaint and charming setting which we decided to settle in. I sought work there with no success for some time. I worked at Mail Boxes Etc. for a month or two, then a group home for less than a month and found my way to a driving and delivery job with the meals on wheels program. It paid $100 a week, plus a few extra bucks I could earn driving the senior shuttle busses but those hours weren't reliable. I greatly enjoyed the delivery work, helping lonely but warm and appreciative elderly shut-ins with their nutrition needs in dirt poor and rural Kittitas County. After I got nabbed for a speeding ticket that cost me half a month's pay I had to move on. I took a seasonal job as a loss prevention detective at a ski resort that paid triple what meals on wheels could.

As the ski season drew to a conclusion I thought I had failed. I decided to return to the Navy to pick up my career where I left off. The Navy would take me back but limited my rating options to jobs in the engine room. I could not return as a Boatswain because there were too many in the Navy at the time. I argued with the Navy recruiter in the recruiting station where an Air Force recruiter overheard the conversation. The Air Force promised a paycheck in less than three weeks. I joined the Air Force reserves. I opted for work as a combat arms training and maintenance (CATM) specialist. I knew weapons and how to teach so it seemed a good fit.

To qualify as a CATM specialist you have to first complete Security Forces qualifications. So I went to the combined law enforcement and airbase ground defense course at Lackland Air Force Base, Texas. I was a squad leader at the school house and graduated in the top ten percent, winning what they call a "distinguished graduate" award. I also testified against a classmate in a fraternization case that broke near the end of the course. It was a matter of integrity, not something I enjoyed. I didn't run to the authorities to tattle, but as the questions were raised I was the only one who broke ranks and spoke the truth to corroborate a report by another. I thought that person's courage to bring forth the report should not be rewarded with a wall of silence that would then result in their integrity being questioned. It was a tough choice I thought would result in my blacklisting in the Security Forces. It did not.

While back in Washington waiting for my CATM course to begin I was given full time temporary work with the Air Force, in part for recognition of my integrity and trust my leadership had in me after the school house incident. They helped me connect with local police departments, Boeing and Microsoft hiring managers. I chose Microsoft where I would work as a kind of 911 operator. I learned how to multitask, gained some high tech computer skills and began researching colleges. I witnessed the Y2K event fizzle from my control room, and the World Trade Organization Riots. I climbed Mount Saint Helens with some coworkers and took side work at Chateau Ste. Michelle in the Columbia Valley in courtesy services. I learned a little about wine there, to this day Columbia Valley is still my favorite wine region. I try to always keep at least one bottle from the Ste. Michelle in the house for a special occasion like receiving an important guest.

I learned to value security too. All of my land based work had been seasonal or very limited in terms of benefits. Microsoft was being sued (by the government!) and stock prices were under pressure forcing cutbacks in support departments like my own. Just before I got a notice of a layoff at Microsoft, I had received word that the civil service wanted me to join them full time and on a permanent basis in California. I drove to Temecula, California where I rented a well-appointed apartment and began to work at March Air Reserve Base. I enrolled in Embry Riddle Aeronautical University and I was soon sidelined by mysterious headaches.

For months my doctors tried to determine the causes. Pinched nerves? An aneurysm? They never figured it out and as suddenly as the headaches had come on they stopped. While the doctors investigated my ailment I was not allowed to be armed so I worked in the back office. I could have stayed home and ignored work; no one would have said anything but it's not my way. I found a way to be useful and became known as a top notch administrator. As soon as I was medically cleared to return to work I was promoted, given awards for my hard work and landed a higher graded position in a more challenging field. That job was in military intelligence with the 28th Infantry Division, Pennsylvania National Guards at Fort Indiantown Gap, just north of Annville.

I drove across the country, I would not recommend that with everything you own in tow. I was chased by a tornado across north Texas. I was lucky to find a motel to hole up in in time to watch a string of twisters roll by on the television. I didn't find souvenirs along the way to make that kind of aggravation worthwhile.

Working for the Army was easier than getting to Pennsylvania. The Army had much lower standards for everything when compared to the Air Force so it was easy to impress them. I rarely felt I had "worked" a day in the Army. I had a lot of fun until 9/11 happened and al-Qaeda sucked the fun out of being a military guy. I was working in the National Guard headquarters joint emergency operations center when it happened. I was having my morning coffee and was the first to notice. I alerted the leadership and began pulling checklists from dusty files when the second plane hit. I declared to my supervisor Tom Maloney "this isn't an accident" and "no matter who did this, where going to Iraq." I had learned to sometimes read the divine and see things in the patterns of history and events unfolding. I had developed keen instincts for world events. I knew that I would be going on the first deployment I could get and that by doing so I would gain the benefit of being exempted from going to Iraq for a long term deployment.

I volunteered to go to the first mission that was announced, it happens to have been a relative cake-walk, but quite ugly in its own way. I was to work in Bosnia-Herzegovina, in an intelligence shop supporting stabilization force rotation twelve (SFOR-12). I hated Bosnia. The place smelled awful, the people weren't particularly warm or interesting and their language was unpleasant. I worked the night shift and my health suffered some. But there was a great benefit to making this trip; I met Alvie, a special friend who would become both hero and brother to me.

When I returned from Bosnia I left the Army and returned to the Air Force as a recruiter. I recruited for two years before moving into education and training management as an orders clerk and test proctor. It wasn't long before I was entrusted with more responsibility and became the lead guidance counselor. The Air Force shrank my career field and I had to find a civilian job. I combined my experiences, education and training to take a unique counterintelligence position at the National Institute of Standards and Technology (NIST).

My military career could have ended in 2009 but I finally made good on my attempt to reenlist with the Navy which I first attempted in 1998. I'm an *Ox*, it can take me significant time to get someplace but tenacity and patience usually pays off.

Going back to the Navy meant a return to intelligence work that would well compliment my counterintelligence position with the NIST. It would also mean an epic battle for justice in the face of bigotry fought with angry letters through my elected representative's office. I've won a small victory at the time of this writing and being a *Scorpio* I'm enjoying a bit of vengeance having embarrassed and forced an Admiral to quickly reverse a position he spent three months arriving at.

That is a quick summary of my career. If it seems a bit of a meandering tale, it is. If some details are missing, feel free to ask me about them. I excluded some things that have been discussed already, or will be discussed elsewhere and to protect the privacy of individuals and sensitive or classified information. Next I want to discuss a few careers I considered and make a couple of suggestions that I hope will help you.

Considered, Not Attempted

I never really knew what I wanted to be when I grew up, I was unsure of what would be satisfying and what would make my family happy and proud. In the Chinese family ethic and tradition what people think of you is quite important. We are what we do, so what you choose to do can determine to great extent what you kind of person you are or just as importantly, are perceived to be. Men spend most of their time working it seems and thus draw a great deal of their identity from their career. This means a career is no small choice. Someone who is great at what they do, as my heroes were, blend life and work seamlessly and they truly become what they do. Confucius once said "Choose a job you love, and you will never have to work a day in your life."

When I was considering what I would do I was forced to take into account a number of practical considerations. I had no real choices, the military or restaurant janitor or maybe a cash register operator. This was no choice. When I was in a position to make some choices in Washington, these were limited by building on what I had already done and attempting to gain some generalized education credentials. Since I began college with the Air Force I built on my Air Force training. The Air Force had enrolled me in a Criminal Justice program so I worked on that and a locally available, affordable technical management four year degree. When I had moved on to Army Intelligence I changed to an affordable human resources oriented degree, and that helped me get human resources work.

I haven't really had the luxury of many choices; it was adapt using the resources at hand or flounder. Sink or swim. Move forward or fall behind. My decisions have been driven by practical considerations and the guiding principle *be like water*. I don't know what I'd have done if I was given the chance to choose. I hope this is a problem that all my children must face, what to do with the freedom to choose a path from infinite opportunities.

One thing I wish I had tried is marine biology. If I had the financial freedom to explore that I would have but with commitments to the reserve military to make ends meet and being responsible to another person for my share of expenses, I couldn't be gone at sea for months on end doing research. If I had the time to pursue a psychology or social work program which require more than double the time I've put into college so far, I would have enjoyed that work. I greatly enjoyed the college guidance counselor position I held for three years with the Air Force and I was good at it.

Some things I would not have sought to do include lawyer, banker or doctor. Lawyers require complete suppression of the self, or abandonment of principles. If we are what we do, this career choice is the ethical and moral equivalent of a prostitute. You peddle lies instead of pleasure and debase yourself and your face for a client's sake. Bankers are destroying our country and contribute little. Our bankrupt monetary system and financial structures are built on lies and victimizing the desperate or the dumb to make a gain on a margin.

Doctors are terrific however; I would not be able to handle the anatomy training. I can't dissect a person. People are too important to me and I've seen the violently killed up close. The horror of their passing resonates with me. I feel empathy towards the dead and could not bring myself to do what a doctor has to gain the title. It is a ghastly trade, thank God for those who are brave enough to do such work.

What Will You Do?

I can't tell you what to do, I would only hope that you are interested enough in something to know what you'd like to do before you are my age (38 at the time of this writing). I will tell you I wish I had learned to fix things and suggest no matter what you do, learn to fix something. I have to hire people for all kinds of repairs, I can fix nautical equipment but I'm at disadvantage in a house repairs. I notice folks who can fix one kind of thing well can fix a lot of things or figure out how. Learn to fix something, anything be it bikes, lawn mowers, computers, it doesn't matter. It can make you a bit more confident perhaps, save you some money, provide a possible secondary income and a hobby to escape from day to day concerns.

Finally and most seriously I cannot stress this enough: do not join the military. Your ancestors have borne more than our kin's fair share of the burden for king and country in wars just and unjust that you should never have to. I would prefer you were an artist, musician, brewer, carpenter, actor, athlete, historian, doctor or social worker. Just about anything but a soldier, sailor or Marine. If you can't resist the lure of uniformed service, the call of adventure and duty consider first the Coast Guard.

They have a military organization but their principle charge is saving lives. Tell me early on if this is what you want to do we'll get you into the academy so you can go in on a leadership management track and not end up a janitor. If you want to punish your body and risk death daily just learning your job, try fireworks technician, professional athlete or stunt man.

If you're wondering what answer I arrived at for the question "what do you want to do when you grow up?" I decided I want to be a good *person*, a good *man*, and a good *dad*. Only you will determine if I have succeeded. I think I've done well so far. What do you want to be? Whatever it is I will be proud, even if it's a lawyer or banker. I understand the draw of those professions. I will do my best to help you start on your journey. I hope this chapter helped you see some of our family values discussed earlier in action. Being adaptable, the value of learning to move up and improve security as well as the importance of a strong work ethic, what it can do for your reputation and how important that reputation is.

Chapter 7

Art & Beauty

"Art begins with resistance - at the point where resistance is overcome. No human masterpiece has ever been created without great labor."

-Andre Gide, French Novelist

While there are many far better qualified to speak about art and beauty than I, there is good reason to discuss it here. In the end of the last chapter I listed a number of career fields I would prefer you explore before considering uniformed service and Artist was the first on that list. Art is an important humanity which can help improve our existence. I use art in a broad sense to mean traditional forms of painting, sculpture and music but also performance and literary arts such as the theatre, film, poetry and novels. New forms or approaches to art that come to our attention from time to time might also be included. I sometimes use art to describe any endeavor or act undertaken or performed by a master who has so refined his craft that it becomes an emotional or transcendent experience to witness the act or product. Feats performed by a master that cannot be undertaken by a novice, or understood by a layperson might fall under this definition as in the lightning quick lethal power of a martial artist in motion. Just about any endeavor can be refined into an art form, beauty can be found almost anywhere.

My own knowledge of art is limited to that of a casual appreciator. Because I have not excelled at or mastered anything, producing art is a challenge for me. I am a good storyteller and I can doodle with a pencil but that's about it. I am only concerned with mastering myself at this point of my life and appreciating the art of others and the beauty that can be found in life. Not all art is beautiful, not everything that is beautiful is art. Beauty can be imperceptible as in the love between two people you pass in the park. The labor of love that goes into maintaining the relationship between two people can be an art. Art is the work of man, beauty the divine.

Art can be an important way to know ourselves and each other. Because it springs from us, it reveals us. Honest art is an intimate portrait of the artist and might be the most important record of human existence once we are gone. Art is an expression of our passions, desires, fears, questions, love, frustrations and other facets of personalities and experiences. Through art we describe our place in the world, our perceptions and interactions with it and each other. We share ourselves through art.

Communication can be an art form and this brings us to this book. While not rising to the level or art, it does pay homage to it. Communication is becoming an underappreciated art form in the *information age;* data and information are often substituted and mistaken for communication. Too much of what passes for communication today filters through technology and is bereft of humanity. It often becomes one sided, narcissistic and shallow. People post short quips on their web pages for their "friends" or "followers". People on their phones or computers are frequently doing other tasks, failing to be polite and give the folks on the other end of their technology their full attention. Sadly people have come to expect no less. In another time this would be intolerable.

Research has shown that many employers rate communication skills above all others when selecting candidates. It can be a tie breaker or set you head and shoulders above rivals when seeking a position or promotion. It matters not how smart you are or how much you know if you can't communicate those ideas in an acceptable way which means at a minimum politely, preferably with emotional intelligence and proper timing as well. This is a skill worth developing not only for career but also for our personal relationships.

Take the time to go to see someone you need to communicate with, carve the time out of your schedule to speak to them face to face if you want to be sure you're understood. The person you visit feels important and knows how important what you want to talk about is. Don't underestimate the power of a face to face meeting. Pay attention to who you are with now, don't worry about sending updates to the world about what the people you are with are doing while you're standing next to them fumbling with a camera or phone or other device.

The dearth of real complete communication which is participative and shared, rich in context, layered and honest is a large part of what this book is about. Instead of leaving you banalities on a website I'm leaving you something more like a written note, a collection of letters and a connection to yourself through our shared history and experiences, a time a three year old will not remember.

A hand written note is another rare communication tool. Second only to face to face contact, a hand written note is quite personal and appropriate for a thank you, or invitation. Hand written words can more delicately communicate emotion and tone with the skill of your hand. One of your mother's favorite things is a hand written note or letter; I love the ones she puts in my lunches. Regretfully my handwriting is dreadful. I must be very patient and keep hand written notes short. With superior handwriting skills you can write a lengthier letter by hand to suite the situation. Women especially appreciate a hand written love letter, they are suitable as gifts and if accompanied by sweets or flowers then doubly so.

My father had terrific hand writing, he tried to pass this skill to me but without explaining it – he barked impatiently at me which made it difficult to learn. It is a skill worth investing some energy in developing. Make sure you develop a distinctive signature which can make a positive or negative impression of you depending on its workmanship, like anything else you do in life. We judge people and their work by its appearance, it's the reality of life we are visual creatures. Mastery of almost any endeavor can make it an art form, if you are open to and infused with the divine it can become beauty. Will you present yourself to the world artfully and contribute to the beauty in the world or mar it with callous disregard for man and the divine?

Chapter 8

Knowing God

"I cannot help thinking the best way of knowing God is to love many things. Love this friend, this person, this thing, whatever you like, and you will be on the right road to understanding him better."

– Vincent van Gogh

I didn't speak much about the divine, Gods and religion until the Art section. There are many ways to know God. Through art some may find the divine within us and it might be one of the ways most readily accessible to you from an early age and thus one way you might have experience with. Attempting to know God is a search for answers. It's why we have religions. But modern religions are the work of politicians and the priest classes who have changed the truly simple understanding of God into a complex maze of mysteries the priests alone are supposedly in possession of the means to decipher. Religion is not ethics or morality. You can be irreligious and ethical, noble and moral. Those are distinct if related philosophical pursuits.

As you know I think of myself as a spiritual orphan. In the western world, religion is largely separated from our public lives. In the eastern world, the divine and invisible unknowable is often openly acknowledged and even interacted with. The eastern perspective is perhaps a more mythic orientation; the divine is all around us and is more fully incorporated into daily life. In the west, religion is something to do on Sunday and some of the big holidays. All too often in both worlds, it teaches only who to hate and some rationalization to do so. Again all too often it is simply the will of God to hate the 'others'. For me as a young man this was an early turn off from organized religion. Before I left home and entered the world I had abandoned the search for God at least temporarily, I was busy.

Before I describe my current understanding I have to share the path I took to get there. I began my search in my mother's Mormon church where I was told that black people are black because there color is a mark put on them by God to warn good white people that the dark person is evil or cursed and not to be trusted. Even in the 1970s when I was a child the church barred people of color from the priesthood and in the past it had barred them from even joining. In Hawaii where many of us are brown to a degree or another, the prohibition on non-whites was a non-starter, so these rules were loosened in Hawaii.

I looked at the Mormon faiths parent sect, Christianity and found its problems are too numerous to begin to dissemble. Their many bibles approve of the institution of slavery. They suggest rape is agreeable in some cases. The Christian faith is itself a sect of Judaism and is based on an acknowledged heresy. Worshipping Jesus is a violation of the first commandment, no matter which version of the Ten Commandments you might be using. The Christian canon has been so heavily edited and so much of what could be understood to be original has been discarded in favor of establishing Jesus as a divinity and not a heretical rabble rouser. More curious is what was left in the books widely recognized as canon (like what Lot and his daughters do).

Going back then to Judaism you find still more trouble, including with the Ten Commandments. Why would an all-powerful deity be jealous? Why would he be so easily roused to anger and vengeance? There are human frailties which rise from our weaknesses. Why would God contract with a tribe to murder and slaughter whole other races of people? The story of Job is a terrifying story about God destroying a poor man to settle a bet with a drinking buddy (the devil). This is widely acknowledged by biblical scholars as one of the more disturbing mysteries in the bible.

I never looked at Islam until I began my military career after I had already found the divine and so it did not figure into my search. Though my father's religion, the Baha'i faith did. The Baha'i faith has its origins in Persia; Islam is from the nearby Arabian Peninsula. The Baha'i faith is a small but still active faith in Iran (formerly Persia) and elsewhere in the world. The two religions are not otherwise related or influential in my understanding of God.

I looked at my father's parents for guidance. His mother Rebecca was a catholic but my grandfather followed Shenism which no one cared to explain to me. I observed as a small boy the burning of fancy paper money to my departed great grandfather, several uncles and Rebecca. I had participated in many large feasts but most of the rituals were bizarre or officiated in Cantonese (our clan's Chinese dialect) which I was never taught. New Years and birthdays I understood, I loved the fireworks and the dragons, those were explained to me as these were celebrated outdoors often with drunken relatives who were happy to explain the ritual in English after a few drinks.

For everything else I wanted to learn about Chinese religion I had to turn to the library and Hawaiian sources. I found Taoism and Confucianism. Both offered a more natural freedom from some angry uber-being waiting for you to make a mistake for which he might turn you into a pillar of salt, murder your family or otherwise punish your clan for generations. This is how I saw God as a young boy. God was a fickle, intoxicated and meddling monster that might destroy me if I failed to do right by him even while what was right was never clear. If he was such a thing I would have no need for him; I already had violent angry and unpredictable people to fear in life and had no need for another.

The Hawaiian religion was essentially wiped out. Remnants of it remained but were little more than ghost stories about night marchers and references to family gods or *Amakua* which might be a hammerhead shark or an owl. A vague notion of a living force tying all things together to the *Aina* or land was a part of all the public school curriculum which skirted the tale of how the natives ate their white discoverer, Captain Cook my favorite explorer.

Later as a teen in study of martial arts as philosophy I had gained a sense for the invisible through my own body's movements. I could sense and perceive changes in my body and the area around me through focus, breathing and motion. Studying Tai-Chi, which began in community college before joining the Navy, I became open to the divine which would be helpful later. When I got on that bus in Chicago to head to Navy Boot camp I wore a small *taijitu* on a chain around my neck. It's commonly known as the yin-yang usually associated with Taoism. I've never worn another religious symbol.

I mention the Navy here because it was only when I had long forgotten about God distracted by the needs of day to day tasks that suddenly it was there. A glimpse of the divine was found in something of no significance to the world.

It was 1996 and I was somewhere in the Mediterranean aboard the *USS Enterprise*. She sailed towards a supply ship on a near parallel course, drawing nearer slowly in a well-rehearsed dance fraught with hazards to begin a vital but routine underway replenishment. The Enterprise had been conducting flight operations over enemy territory and must take on aviation fuel for the jets to continue operations ordered by the President.

Michael Chandler

I was standing watch as a lookout on the starboard bridge wing some seventy feet in the sky. It is a beautiful sunny day, not a cloud in sight and the sea was a brilliant azure. As I stare, detached and bored across the sea towards the horizon something catches my eye just off the starboard bow between us and the supply ship, a plume of mist from a whale surfacing for a breath. Then another and another, soon a dozen or more sperm whales are spotted and others aboard the ships begin to take notice. Grown men, fighting men begin to point and a hushed chatter briefly rises before all go silent to watch the animals.

The whales are taking short breaths popping up in rapid succession, mothers with calves and large bulls over fifty feet long all preparing to dive to evade us. We slow a bit to avoid overtaking them too quickly and watch as their misty plumes form a cloud. A rainbow appears between the ships over the great whales and all aboard marvel at the miracle of light as the whales vanish into the darkness below. The rainbow lingers for a few moments. I was transported off the decks of that ship, away from war and the fatigue that soaked my bones. I was connected peacefully to the whole of the universe for a few moments.

Soon the ships resumed their work, smoothly with a light and reverent tone. For a long time that was my happiest memory eclipsing every small joy that I had known before it. It was the first time I cared to acknowledge God or cared to contemplate his nature as something other than an angry and indifferent master of the universe. I had always loved whales and sea creatures but never God. It might be a defect of mine. But soon thereafter, as if to cement this memory forever in my heart a port visit to Haifa, Israel our next stop teaches me that peace and happiness can be found in unexpected places even in tragedy and the faces of the forgotten.

When we anchor, I plan to engage in a typical day or two of carousing and touring. The obligatory tourist stops for memories I'll wash away with a pint or three as the sun sets. On the morning of our arrival as I rise from my slumber something draws me away from my friends to the hanger deck. A small group has gathered but I don't know what they're doing. They're mostly older sailors and the chaplain is there too, they're all in grungy work jeans or tattered khakis, a few in shorts and all sport loose t-shirts or tank tops. An announcement over the 1MC (a ships public address system) says that the chaplains group is mustering now and will depart in fifteen minutes. I mosey on over to investigate.

The jolly and rotund minister tells me that he's looking for hands to help with a small project over the week we are in port with a French order of nuns 'Maison du Sacre Couer' (house of the sacred heart). I thought of the

The Ox and Scorpio

French of course only as surrender monkeys and a class I got a 'D' in once. I thought of nuns as an anachronism from medieval times, a cult that might be imitated at the renaissance faire and certainly out of place in the Jewish homeland. The sun peered in at me through the open hangar bay doors and *the glistening sea told me* to "join them."[21] And so I went with the pudgy old sailors and their priest. It was another beautiful sunny day. It wasn't hot or unpleasant and a cool shore breeze gently swept away any hint of fatigue when it threatened.

We arrived after a short bus ride at a sand colored church compound with a rusted iron gate. Inside we were given a tour of the place what was explained to me as a refuge for children orphaned, abandoned or mutilated by terrorist bombs, land mines, snipers or other Israeli-Palestinian conflict related horrors. Dozens of children, clean and very well cared for, of all ages were here and I had to fight back tears as a disabled infant smiled up at me from the tiny crib that was her entire world. She had one good hand and she reached out to grab my finger, tugging as fiercely at my heart with smiling eyes as at my finger with her tiny hand.

Her parents were both killed by a rocket recently and she had survived but was alone in the world now. I was able to spend some time with her pushing her along in what could best be called a stroller. I made airplane or car engine noises as I pushed her around the yard fueled by laughter that didn't stop until she had finally become exhausted and happily drifted off into a nap. I held her for a moment and gave her back to a sister who gently took her away. After the morning meet and greet with the children we went to work repairing a jungle gym and playground equipment. I fixed the sand box whose framing timbers had crumbled away. I fit new ones and poured fresh sand in to it after removing what was left of the old.

The old sailors made good use of me moving concrete for a walk that had crumbled. I was the youngest and so I hauled tons of concrete in a wheelbarrow from a cement mixer out front into the compound carefully maneuvering that thing into place so as not to waste any of the cement bought with donations. We lunched with the kids too, cheeseburger sliders the nuns had made, a great pile of them on a silver platter three feet across and a second full of fries! It was ridiculous but I enjoyed it. I washed mine down warm grape soda. To this day grape soda makes me think of those little kids smiling alone in the desert protected by the nuns.

---

[21] Alvie asked me "who do you attribute this message to? God or some other spirit?" I think now that it was my grandmother Rebecca.

We worked the next day too on still more projects and played some with the children or read to them. There they were 'broken' and abandoned seemingly without hope or prospects reliant on strangers for life in the middle of a simmering war and yet they were happy, content and at peace. I was a miserable wretch, slaving away day to day exhausted wishing for sleep hoping for the cruise to end but fearing the boredom of what might come next. I wondered what these kids knew that I didn't and how they could be so joyful without full use of their bodies. I was embarrassed for ever feeling sorry for myself or angry about anything in life that didn't work out how I had wanted it to. I didn't understand it but I was seeing God in their smiling eyes and they had healed me and helped me far more than I could ever hope to have helped them.

Fast forward some fifteen years and I can tell you my understanding of God is akin to the deist tradition. I understand God to be a force most easily approximated as a *law of consequence* terrible and benign at once, Yin and Yang. In practical application I am a Taoist believing that "the way that can be named is not the true way"[22], that "inaction can be the most creative action"[23] and nothing is forever, not life, nor perhaps even death. Taoism is a sect of Shenism with its tens of thousands of 'gods' which are more human than divine as are the squabbling gods of the Greek, Roman and Norse pantheons. In the Taoist tradition there is no real creator dictator god as in the monotheistic faiths, if there is such a god it is of no consequence to a Taoist.

In the Deist tradition, Natural Law and Nature's God (the one in the Declaration of Independence) ought to be obeyed and worshipped but there is not an organized priesthood interpreting God's will or controlling the keys to salvation. I see God in nature and in children, in the sun and sky, the earth and the sea as the ancients did. I believe that would make me something of a Deist, but I don't care. I don't have to belong to any club, cult, sect or tribe to know God or his law.

There is limited value in the hand-me-down religions of old. They have been corrupted by *priestcraft* and though useful in delivery of social services and solace to some in need, many churches have become businesses. This doesn't mean you can't benefit from participating with a church, after all in Haifa I was working with nuns and a Catholic priest in the Holy Land when I got the best perspective on God one could ask for.

---

[22] Loose translation from the *Tao-Te Ching*.
[23] Ibid

Searching for God might be a worthwhile pursuit. For me knowing God was worth the Navy and all of its horrors, the helicopter crash, the endless watches and all of the other glimpses of hell. Like art, spirituality and the quest for God can bring some beauty into your life and can help us find strength. While organized religions are not for me, they might suite you so I would not discourage you from joining a group or think less of you if you did. I hope you will not think less of me for being spiritually lost, I'm fine.

Knowing God is difficult. Religious knowledge is the hardest to share because so much of it is attained through experiences that are often completely internal and subjective. We use ritual (like travel) and prayer to seek God. Sometimes accidents reveal God to us as in my near death experience. I believe my drowning connected me to the invisible unknowable allowing me, since the whale rainbow and Haifa, the ability to read signs and portents, to see God's law in action.

If you're looking for rules or commandments, tenants or a checklist of "do's and don'ts" to associate with my religious smash-up here are some suggestions.

- Be good
- Use Common Sense
- Be kind treating everyone as or better than you want to be
- Consider inaction
- Avoid excesses
- Maintain a healthy skepticism

For more you'll have to consult the *Tao-Te Ching* and your own ability to reason, always your best guide and most important gift from any creator that might be.

Chapter 9

Augury and Portents

"In the magical universe there are no coincidences and there are no accidents. Nothing happens unless someone wills it to happen."

- William S. Burroughs

If the invisible unknowable is a force of law, with form and structure, then it stands to reason it will have a pattern that can be discerned. One could drive himself mad trying to read the patterns in the universe so I don't recommend trying. There are moments and glimpses you can hope to catch though and with time you may be able to learn to spot them. Some might consider this a function of wisdom and age, experience and training or learning. I don't discount those important tools for making predictive analysis but there is something more in my opinion. There is good reason to develop your instincts and experience, stop, reflect and consider them before acting or making a critical decision like choosing an alliance, taking or seeking a job, beginning a journey or leaving the house that morning. But be open to the invisible and feelings that might warn of peril even if irrational.

I can share a few anecdotes about my own Auguries – used here to mean simply vivid dream pictures of the future not dissecting a bird to read the future in its stomach contents. Portent is used here to mean warnings that come in dreams or sensations or a sequence of events or occurrences that point to danger. These are difficult to give examples of because they are often fleeting momentary realizations and I'm usually nowhere near a pen and paper but thankfully I can act on these things. I'll discuss a few for you before wrapping up this short chapter. I can't talk about all of them, some haven't yet come to pass and so I can't corroborate them at the time of this writing. I failed to act on a few that might have affected other people and should they learn of these warnings I failed to share they might become upset.

One of my most recent portents happened in 2009. I was getting ready to begin my current job. It was suggested to me that I take the metro rail in to the Department of Commerce headquarters building which is at the end of the red line meaning I wouldn't even have to go outside and risk being caught in the rain. I could enter the building through the basement and avoid famous epic traffic jams along the D.C. beltway, I-270 and the Washington Parkway. I had only driven part of this route before to Gaithersburg where I interviewed and would actually be working but I had never driven this route into D.C. My few trips through D.C. were only to get to Virginia. So the train would eliminate the risk of getting lost too.

I despise D.C. but I was willing to give it a chance for the high paying new job. I even interviewed for a job that was in the Reagan building with the Department of Homeland Security just across the street from the Herbert C. Hoover building (HCHB- the Department of Commerce). I did not relish the experience of taking what I had heard would be three hours to get some 22 miles from the actual job site, which was over two hours away from our hundred year old house. Gas prices were insane and parking wouldn't be reimbursed if it was available and there was no guarantee it would be. If the orientation day ended on schedule I might be able to be home by seven pm. I was told the metro rail would save me hours and cost less than half as much. I would still have to drive into Germantown or Frederick but I would be able to avoid the worst of the drive. I thought about it for only a few moments. Something told me to deal with it - get in my car and just make the best of it.

I wasn't being lazy to avoid trying something new; I was excited to try new things associated with this new civilian job, my first in over ten years. I wanted to adapt to the new culture I would be immersed in as a D.C. area worker and commuter. The day I drove in for my interview I was excited that there radio news stations dedicated to discussing matters of concern to the federal workforce I was joining.

The drive in was miserable. I was barely on time and nearly hit several times. I found parking though and I managed to get through the worst orientation event ever. It was June 22, 2009 my first day on the job with Commerce and the day of the worst accident in D.C. metro history. The red line had a train collision that killed nine people. I heard about it on my way home on my car radio. The crash had worsened traffic on my route. I got home late but happy to be home uninjured.

Many months later my boss convinced me to take a trip in on the repaired red line to meet and greet the director of our division. I sensed no specific danger and went. I had a good day. My boss knew the rail system and the D.C. streets so it was easy to get a good lunch and interesting to meet her former office partners for a Starbucks. Several months later my boss asked me to take another trip into D.C. on the rail for a short meeting. I was ready to go but I sensed danger and rescheduled the meeting. I heard the next day the train had another accident during the evening rush killing another person.

Missing one accident on the train? I could chalk that up to coincidence but two accidents, on the same stretch of track I'd be on, at the times I could expect to have been on it with one of those accidents being the worst ever, what are the odds?

Some might suggest, quite rationally that my decision to drive was instinct based on knowledge of D.C. infrastructure conditions and incompetent management endemic in transit agencies and Washington government in general. I didn't possess detailed knowledge but a general sense from my global situational awareness as an intelligence analyst and amateur social scientist. As an adult I avoided public transit generally shunning it but I never feared it. As a child in Hawaii I often depended on it, transferring twice from home to school during my year at Junior Achievement[24]. I was comfortable with public transit but simply preferred to have my own vehicle in case of emergency. I'm not a control freak but I do like to be ready.

I suggest my brush with death gifted me awareness for its presence. I live in what I see as a magical universe unlike most westerners I'm comfortable saying that. Most folks would privately admit to believing in ghosts and as many go to church on Sunday to ask supernatural beings for assistance in personal matters yet dramatically fewer are likely to include the supernatural world in their daily commute planning or other mundane matters. We're trained to rely on the eyes, science and rational thought not feelings or intuition. It is wrong to see science and the mythical as diametrically opposed or mutually exclusive.

I interpreted the crashes as a sign to stay out of D.C. and worry of some great calamity looming. I fear when I leave the D.C. area it will experience a significant tragedy and that if I foolishly linger I will be caught in it. There are other things have happened that tell me D.C. is not for me.

---

[24] After failing my first year of middle school I was enrolled in a Junior Achievement program 1.5 hours away by bus.

The Ox and Scorpio

When driving on I-270 I was struck from behind three times. The first was a tap during bump and go, not worth looking at. The second was a significant bump worth checking out and which I spent time in the nurses' station getting checked for injury and the most recent sent me to the emergency room with concussion like symptoms. These injuries are warnings to get the heck out of the area as far as I'm concerned. I've responded with an increased aggressiveness in my Pennsylvania area job searching. I see a pattern here which points to a significant if not lethal fourth accident next year which will be my fourth with the Dept. of Commerce.

Not every connection to the unknowable invisible is about death. There are benign and amusing auguries too. I was at sea in 1999 aboard an inter-island tug hauling freight to Oahu. John Elway and the Denver Broncos were winning the Super Bowl but I was at sea. I dreamt that night of the strangest thing. In the dream I was standing in the snow at ski resort in a high mountain pass. I had a brown hat and black and white flannel coat. I was with a tall thin fellow and we were patrolling the ski resort on foot. When I woke I had to laugh it was so implausible. I had just left the mainland and wished never to return, winter nights in the pacific were cool enough for me, and never would I be on a mountain top for any reason.

A little over a year later I had that ski resort job quite by accident. I had not intended to settle near the mountain. Truthfully Ellensburg was nowhere near the mountain. I commuted over thirty miles each way daily. Nor was Ellensburg my intended location. When I moved to Washington my destination was Moses Lake some 50 miles further east. The ski resort job was dreadful, but the money was good and I met some nice folks. I worked with a tall thin fellow named Adam who lived in Ellensburg but whom I had not known until taking the job at the mountain. Someone bought me a black and white coat and a brown hat. Someone took a picture of me there on the mountain in the hat and coat and I realized then how I should pay a great deal more attention to my dreams and share them frequently with others.

But the universe doesn't revolve around me, far from it. The universe acts on me to the benefit of others in some cases as it does us all. Case in point, in 1997 the Enterprise was back from the shipyard and pier side. I was just waiting for my separation paperwork to move through the bureaucracy and was on my way out. One night during a storm I found myself up reading. It was some god awful work book that I had no interest in. I could not get to sleep despite the weather. Storms usually lull me to sleep almost instantly. One of my favorite things about Pennsylvania is the ferocity of the thunder we get. Before moving to PA, I've never encountered anything like it. So there I was alone[25] in the dark with a wretched book. It was after midnight. I tossed the book into the laundry pile beside the bed and grabbed my keys.

I drove onto the highway in the downpour determined to drive just a few miles hoping that would relax me. The roads were empty at that late hour and the rain limited visibility to just a few dozen yards. I was finally beginning to relax and thought "I'll take the next exit and turn around." I was coming around a bend and there I spotted a car in the left shoulder with its hazards on. You shouldn't do what I did. I stopped hoping this person wasn't a serial killer or a robber. There were reports of people being set up and robbed by folks pretending to be broken down on the highway like this but I believe thieves and malcontents avoid bad weather being uncomfortable with nature. I reasoned that nature sees through the masks worn by people to hide their weakness, it cuts through all that rendering them naked and equal to their victims, it forces them to feel human. To be a rogue, you can't have empathy for humanity. Nature forces the villain to confront their own frailty and they fear this more than anything.

An honest man does not fear the rain, but a thief does.

So with this thought in my head I decided it must be someone in trouble. I got out of the car and approached the driver side. There was a frightened young black woman. I can only imagine what she was thinking having seen the recent news stories that I had. I thought seeing me there in my black hoody staring down at her from behind my bushy eyebrow must have been a less than reassuring site. I moved slowly and tapped on her window. She rolled it down a crack and fearfully declared "my car died". I didn't think I could help, at this point in my life I couldn't fix a sandwich but I asked her to pop the hood and I took a look. The only thing I could figure out that was wrong was the car was older than I was.

I asked her through the cracked window if she would like a lift to a gas station or pay phone (cell phones were not widely available then). She reluctantly agreed, and I helped her into my car. She didn't say much. I got her to a gas station then waited while she made a call. She came back to my car apparently deciding to trust me and said that she couldn't reach anyone.

---

[25] My roommate was away in Chicago visiting family after shooting a hole in the floorboard a few days prior. The bullet, a .357 magnum round, had ricochet through my pillow on the floor where I slept and lodged itself in the bi-fold closet door. Our neighborhood was such that no one had noticed the gunshot or reported it. It was a source of some tension between us and soon after I moved out to live with Dave and Sara where I remained until flying home to Hawaii a few weeks later.

She asked me if I could drive her home, pleading that it was only a short distance. I agreed of course and took her home directly. I wished her luck and watched as she got into her apartment door safely. She waved as she closed the door and I drove home.

I never got her name, I wouldn't recognize her if I saw her and I don't know why the universe had me out there in the rain. I've never done that before or since. It's dangerous and shouldn't be done. Maybe she'll go on to cure cancer or be a good mother to the guy who does? Maybe she's just a normal kid who needed a break and deserved one. I was only out there for about fifteen minutes before I came across her, what are the odds? I know she appreciated the help and I'm glad she didn't run into a bad guy. I slept well when I got home.

On other occasions an augury or portent shed light on the future for me with time to act to change my path. When the planes were crashing on 9/11, I knew we were heading into Iraq, no matter who was responsible. Yes many wise analysts were thinking this soon after the attack, but I knew it, and proclaimed it as it was happening. I also saw clearly that I would be going there with the Army unless I jumped on the Bosnia mission that had been in the works for two years.

I first learned about the Bosnia mission in May of 2001. I was told during the interview for the intelligence job "you might have to go to Bosnia with if you join this unit, I needed to tell you because a lot of people are afraid to go and its caused a lot of people to run away and transfer out" to which I laughed "I've been to Bosnia before it's not so bad send me." I got the job of course but was not put on the list to go. Even after the 9/11 attacks I wasn't on the list of people who were being ordered to go to Bosnia. I was on a glide path to war in Iraq and I felt that serious injury waited for me there and great change. I don't know who I'd have become had I gone, but that person cannot be as I chose another path.

Two weeks before the battalion moved out for Bosnia I was given a last chance. In an unheard of move the General sent out a personal email and a spreadsheet with information about all the vacancies he had left to fill for his mission. It was a plea for volunteers. There was a hole for an intelligence sergeant. I told my boss it was my intention to go. He said to me "are you sure, I know you're convinced that you'll be sent to Iraq if you don't get on this trip but I can be pretty sure you won't have to go anywhere if you don't want to. It's easy to get out of these things" but I was only angered by his suggestion that I would ever shirk my responsibilities when the call of duty came. I said "to hell with you I'll see you in nine months if you're still here." I packed up my stuff and put in my leave without pay (LWOP) paperwork, went home and prepared over the next two weeks to be gone for nine months.

Turns out I was right. I escaped the Iraq mission without trying. When I returned many had gone from my unit but there was a lag in need, everyone anticipated a short war – I knew better. I moved into recruiting and there I was immune to mobilizations and made twice as much as I did in intelligence. Several waves of call ups came and until I moved out of recruiting I was safe. Many who I had known before had gone and some died.

Then each year there was a minor scare of an Afghanistan call up. I hadn't feared Afghanistan at all; it seemed unpleasant and stupid to go so I didn't want to go but I didn't fight it. I'm happy I didn't go, I would have returned only to be told I'm not needed anymore in the downsizing initiative that savaged my career field with the Air Force. I never got any inkling from Afghanistan, just a gray hazy ambivalence from the universe. Nothing I could decipher just three years, three warnings of possible deployment there each time it seemed the likelihood of being sent was greater, each time I wished more not to go.

After two trips to Bosnia, I wonder if a third is in the cards. It would fit the pattern. I have believed for some time that there is one more deployment in store for me before I retire. I've shared this with your mother. For a long time it figured prominently in our discussions about whether to remain in the military beyond 2009 or to leave all together. I've watched carefully for some sign but have perceived nothing. Honestly I'm distracted, there is a lot going on right now with your baby brother about to be born..

I think my new unit, a Navy construction battalion or "Sea Bee" unit, doesn't know exactly what to do with me. I have a good feeling about them, they're rambunctious and have said they're trying to restore the fun lost since 9/11. My favorite color is green; unlike most of the Navy the Sea Bees wear predominately green uniforms. When World War II was winding down my dad was assigned to an (Army) construction battalion where he quietly rode out the end of that conflict. So for me I now expect I'll watch my career quietly fade away too as I've missed every war I've been in before.

Yes that sounds odd but it's true. When I joined in 1995, my class was the last to get credit for joining during the "Gulf War Era." I just squeaked into being classified as a Gulf War Era Vet which helped me get a federal job. When I sailed off Bosnia the first time the war there was over too, at least most of it was. It had begun to simmer into a ceasefire. When I returned to Bosnia with the Army the peace keeping mission was winding down and the transition period was ending. During my stay there, early in our

The Ox and Scorpio

mission the country held its first unmonitored elections in seven years and it went off without any significant incidents. It was probably a cleaner election that what we have here in the states. There is a funny story attached to those elections that illustrate a total fail of my connection to the invisible that requires props to tell. You don't get to hear that story until you finish college and you buy me a drink. The story requires props to tell correctly, your mother or Alvie can help you with the correct items to have handy for the telling.

My senses aren't precise, I can't pull winning lottery numbers out of the sky but I've found happiness and safety by paying attention to information sources based not in the rational but found in horoscopes, feelings or dreams. Answers given in response to questions shouted to the stars or prayers to the spirits of the departed. I have relied upon and benefited much more from these sources of wisdom than education, training and any rational decision models. When I approached your mother, I was propelled forward towards her awkwardly by something beyond me and look what happened (I feigned confidence with my customary swagger). The universe is a magical place and by my reckoning only a lonely fool would attempt to deny this.

Act II Curtain

"The beginning is the most important part of the work."

- Plato

I love beginnings, I think most people do. They are a delightful mix of anxiety and discovery, a chance to discover new people and rediscover or invent oneself. Collecting beginnings has given me a rich rewarding life both professionally and personally. I took risks and gambled with starting over often but learned how to use what I had learned in the nest as I took flight again and again. It wasn't always pretty and some lessons had to be applied in unexpected ways to survive but I made it work because I had to. Sometimes it wasn't my choice to seek another beginning and I unwisely made it harder than it needed to be, picking fights that didn't need to be fought. I discovered that I can't act without my conscience and morality foremost in making decisions. I believe that was the most important component of my initiation, discovering my understanding of the stoic ethic, morality based on reason and natural law of the cosmos's creator that isn't.

I learned other important things about life and the world too. I learned to identify and appreciate learning opportunities when they come and to take advantage of them, not something I always did well. I got stronger and learned to pick my battles and I was ready to return home to use what I had learned. But this was not in the cards for me. Life is full of surprises, some frightful but some are wellsprings of joy and further surprises. It was just this kind of surprise I closed the last chapter with.

The universe put your mother before me and prodded me to say hello. It was out of character for me at the time to do so. I had just ended a relationship that had gone on too long and I was preparing to return to

Hawaii. I had made a trip to line up a job and the night I met your mother I was hoping to simply avoid notice there tagging along with some friends in a sometimes rough bar. Your mother was hiding with an older girlfriend hiding out too. Before either of us knew what had happened we moved into the hundred year old house, married and soon you were on your way.

But there is another important surprise the universe held in store for me. I could have mentioned Alvie a dozen times already and he might argue he deserves his own chapter. There was no single topic that would do him justice and like your mother, Alvie makes appearances in many places so I will devote a part of this section to him because I met him in the middle of Act II.

Alvie could have been featured in the Hero chapter, he is certainly that. His encouragement and role modeling in this area, helped me to believe I could be a father, like him, of a character far different from that of my own father. I had wanted and planned to be different from my father; nonviolent, present to the greatest extent possible and involved but wasn't sure I had a good bead on how. Alvie showed me how he did it and inspired me to make my own way free of my father's unforgiving shadow.

Once I visited him with your mother for the Rams vs. Redskins game. I brought a pizza and beers and we planned on having a good time. His wife was there to pepper me with questions about my heredity and growing up in Hawaii, nothing unusual, and his kids were running around I think he had three at that time (he has four today). All of a sudden while flipping between games (our game was a real stinker both teams records were 2-10 or something awful) one kid pooped while the other was crying for a piece of pizza. No problem for Alvie the super dad. He changed the one kids diaper, with one hand, while flipping channels, never missing a play – fed the other kid a few bites of his pizza and he managed to get in a sip of his beer, paid attention to my joke and got the freshly diapered kid dressed. All at once! It was like he was an octopus or a father artist.

I could have mentioned him in the artist section too, I've told others when recommending him for advancement that watching him work is a thing of beauty, the man is an artist and his medium is tedious grunt work which he turns into efficient, accurate finished art, in a mere fraction of the time required by three times as many others. It's the kind of work that makes others look good, he is the rare fellow who with the right leaders who listen to him, can make the difference between success and destruction. As a boss I'd choose him over the five next best people any day. Do you know why he is so good at anything he does? Unlike me, he is supremely adaptable and incredibly lazy.

Michael Chandler

He lives the Way and is always like water. He sees the path much clearer than I could ever hope. Don't think by calling him lazy I'm mocking him; lazy people are the producers of some of man kinds greatest achievement and innovations, imagineered in the name of not having to work as hard as I prize working (foolishly – work smarter not harder, my ethic is slightly flawed and my training poor in this regard). Life is better because of people with the lazy work ethic who apply their laziness with unparalleled vigor. He is supremely intelligent too, always forgiving and aware of his own imperfect understanding of the universe and so he has been a terrific partner on the spiritual journey to know God and he could have been mentioned there.

He considers himself an agnostic of sorts, or perhaps 30% deist he once suggested and he is a fan of Taoism. A copy of the *Tao-Te Ching* was something I gifted to him early on in our friendship. I gave him my worn copy of *Catch-22* also upon the occasion of his promotion to Technical Sergeant, the rank I held at the time. I could have mentioned him in my favorite things along with my favorite books; *Catch-22* reminds me of our friendship and his embodiment of subversive wisdom. He had already discovered the pacifist way when I met him and fearlessly gave expression to his mild subversive streak when I was still a naïve believer in the illusions of misapplied patriotism.

When I met Alvie I was only beginning to flirt with the idea of thinking for myself and questioning the establishment powers and message. I would explore independent analysis and read thinks like *Catch-22* not on the official recommended readings lists, Hackworth and Boyd the way a youngster might sneak a peek at forbidden channels when his parents are away or asleep. Alvie was leading the subversive pride parade right down the national mall and I was still in the subversive closet fearing discovery.

Since I met him in the Army, on the way to Bosnia he could have been written about in the career section. Our extensive dialectics helped me arrive at the decision to walk away from the military as a career, ironic or unexpected since I convinced him in 2003 to remain in the military, and to follow me from the Army Guard to the Air Guard. Others quickly realized his gifts and in no time he had obtained a coveted full time guard position, something that took me a bit more than a year to obtain for myself.

If I were to write a chapter about friends, of whom I have few he would be the first to be discussed. Some friendships run the course of a season, serve a specific purpose or are with us only for various reasons but some are worth hanging on to and keeping. In my life I've had two such friends. Alvie and your mother, fortunately the two get along. When I told

Alvie I was very serious about your mother he expressed his concern honestly, worried I was taking it too fast with her. I took her to meet him and he thought she was terrific and told me to go for it, he understood. He didn't have to do that but I was emotionally fragile during this period and I think he knew how much his support would mean to me. He didn't have to be honest with me about his concerns either, that takes courage and trust that is truly rare in those we might call friends. When your mother and I were married a short time later, Alvie would be my best man.

Of course Alvie and I worked in intelligence together so I can't tell you much about that, we're professional spooks, shadow people from a world we despise for its unaccountable excesses, rampant cognitive dissonance and moral vagueness.

So once Alvie helped me woo your mother he would fade a bit into the background. I would check with him from time to time about parenting issues and always marvel at his ability to juggle his commitments and family. I speak with him almost daily about the news, weather, God, kids, fantasy literature, the wives and war. But he has many friends and his focus is his family, as is mine. When you arrived your mother and I were so busy all of a sudden there was almost never time to check in with a friend.

To begin with your arrival took forever! You decided that you would not be delivered in less than 34 hours. I think the final count was 36 hours. And the incompetents at Harrisburg Hospital seemed determined to find a new ways to prolong the experience for your poor mother. She nearly died. Thankfully the surgeon was a master of his craft. He paused during the operation to make a joke waving your arm at me as he delivered you and squeaking "hi daddy" from behind his operating mask for a moment before you were handed to me and he stitched up your mother.

I wept openly at seeing you (and Miranda too) as I presented you to your mom. I was so afraid I would drop you I held you with an iron grip. I gained new strength from the universe as you were placed into my hands. Suddenly I wore the mantle of father. I would no longer be plodding ahead forging a path for myself alone; I would be the captain of our family ship. The weight of your world was squarely on my shoulders. I had the strength thanks to my initiation but mistook that strength alone for complete readiness for fatherhood. The universe held many surprises in store for me and it would not be long before they would begin to be revealed. In four days[26] we made the trip home to the hundred year old house.

      I began Act II naïve, still subject to a number of illusions. Over time I shed them, gaining wisdom instead but remaining true to myself. I increasingly looked at moral and ethical implications of my actions ahead of all other considerations even though as I progressed in my career this would become an increasingly dangerous proposition. I would speak the truth as I understood it and I would dare detractors to attack my iron tower of reason. This doesn't make one popular and might account for my lack of rank at this late date in my career. I sleep well at night and that's what matters to me. I still had a lot to learn when you arrived on the scene. Perhaps the most important thing I learned during my initiation is that I was not as smart as I thought I was.

---

[26] This represents an unusually long stay due to the toll your birth took on your mother.

ACT III
Return

Chapter 10

Near Death Parenting

"It's the friends you can call up at 4 a.m. that matter."

-Marlene Dietrich

As I had written before, I thought I had a good bead on things, thought I was ready and knew enough now to be a dad. I had a role model in Alvie, I had my father's example of what not to do and had steered a course away from his worst features. Knowing a child is educated by what their parents are and not by their words[27] I had lived with my conscience as my guide, even though this has kept me from advancing as well as some of my peers. To my delight and dismay the universe held several lessons and surprises in store for me and your mother who has been with me now for two years before you arrived.

This chapter begins here where you might have just learned your wife is going to have a baby or your first has just arrived, you might be nervous or just exhausted. It's okay, it'll change everything and it's a lot of work but it's a good time and worth all the work. There will be accidents, mistakes will be made but be patient and don't let this little creature signal an end to your primary relationship for which your child owes its existence and upon which its survival depends.

Before becoming a father I thought my parents were idiots. I've since learned to be more forgiving in my assessment of their parenting, especially after suffering my own near death parenting experiences. Yes my parents nearly killed me on at least one occasion but to be fair wrangling two toddlers

---

[27] Paraphrasing Carl Jung

for a young mother (my mom was barely 20 at the time) has got to be tough, especially when you're forced to watch them at an industrial site. **So rule number one, don't take your baby to industrial sites**. If you think you might have had a rough first night with your infant at home, or you're wondering what to expect let me share the tale of your first night out of the hospital home in the hundred year old house.

Babies First Night Home

The first night we got you home from the hospital I had to make three hundred trips up a tall narrow stairwell in our hundred year old house to bring you and your mother, your pack-and-play (crib) diapers, wipes, thermometer, clothes, bandages, water and a million bottles of ointments, snacks and food, bottles and God knows what up the stairs. I thought I was going to die. I hate stairs.

This is why we bought a ranch house in Gettysburg. That and my knee cartilage had long been destroyed by living on an aircraft carrier and on long marches in the Army years before. To make things worse that night your mother couldn't help, she could barely get up the stairs, they were so small and tall it wasn't really something she should be doing but she did it and I ran back up and down a thousand times that first night.

After that exhausting day we got everyone settled in for a good night's sleep which was impossible in the hospital where we lived for a week. You woke up every two hours, but it seemed more like every fifteen minutes. I couldn't sleep because you needed fed or you had pooped or you were cold. So cold in fact that at one point, and I don't know why I checked, but your temperature had dropped enough to make me think you were going to freeze to death!

Your mom thought you felt cold during a feeding or changing and that made sense since you were sleeping next to the drafty hundred year old window. We got a heating pad out and put you in the bed with us to warm you back up and it worked. You finally gave us a good long sleep – turns out you just kept waking us up because you were cold. After that I kept your room at 72 degrees constantly and soon you slept through the night.

Heating bills be damned keep the baby's area at 72 degrees, you can't put a price on a long sleep or a quiet baby. Also, **never wake a baby** – that's easy to do, getting them to sleep again is not. No good reason to wake a baby.

It wasn't long after that you rolled off your changing table (the night before a doctor's appointment) as if trying to convince me that you were indestructible. I can't say who was there in the room with you but I *heard* that you were trying to catch bunny-bun-bun who had fallen off the table first. Lesson here – there are safety straps in the changing table kit – install them and use them, ok? Ok.

Your Big Boo Boo

Your burn accident was entirely my fault. My confidence was deeply shaken by this event. I was shocked and very worried I was doomed to fail as a father. You were in the new grabby stage near Christmas and we were settling in for story time after getting the Christmas tree set up. I put a large steel mug full of just poured hot water and a green tea bag on the table and went to sit with you in my lap. The idea was to read you the Happy Baby Words book and then maybe some Christmas stories.

You grabbed the mug and poured it over you as we sat down. I got you into the shower and we called 911. You rode a helicopter to the best burn unit on earth. This was probably why the divine placed us here just a few months before, otherwise no telling where you might have ended up for care. It was dicey there in the hospital for a week. A big blizzard blew in and there was constant struggle against infection. We got out of the hospital just before the blizzard shut down Baltimore and we were safely snowed in at home. You did get a small infection though and I had to trek through 20" snowfall (I never really needed my 4x4 before but I had almost always owned one) to get to the Rite Aid to pick up antibiotics that quickly killed your infection.

I had to fight with the idiots at John Hopkins who insisted I bring you back or that we shouldn't treat an infection without blood tests at their clinic some thirty five miles away. I *reasoned* with that doctor until she finally agreed to give you the prescription just to get me off the phone. Fight for your kids. Doctors don't have a vested interest, they don't always care. The doctors at JH just wanted to perform surgeries or follow protocols to maximize billable hours.

Before this and similar albeit less serious routine injuries I thought such things only happened to idiots. Being a parent teaches you to be more forgiving. I harshly judged my own parents in particular for my own serious hospitalization which I'll recount here for you.

My Near Death Experience

My first memory is of drowning. I was a toddler, three, almost four years old and sent to the car to retrieve a blanket for my new baby sister. She was cold in the frigid boat house on the pier. The boat house was kept meat locker cold to keep the smell of the place down like a morgue. I pushed the flimsy splintering door open and squinted to see in the harsh sunlight. The door slammed shut behind me and I trotted gaily off to the red corolla my father had recently bought. I retrieved the blanket and ran excitedly back to my family.

The boat house was so close to the edge of the pier that as I came around the bend I tripped over the blanket and into the water ten feet below. I had not yet learned to swim and I sank like a stone wrapped up in the blanket I clung to desperately while trying to cry for help from beneath the waves. I swallowed enough salt water that I soon rested on the bottom, eventually the blanket floated up to tell where I had fallen.

Mom sensed something was wrong, she had finished feeding my sister (Monica) and had thought I would return by then. She told my father and he ran out to look – expecting to find me feeding a pigeon or stray cat that frequented the pier. He walked to the car and saw the blanket was gone. He climbed the steel stair next to the parking lot to ask the dispatcher in the upstairs office if I was in there with playing with the radios or flashlights.

This is where my dad says he panicked and ran down to see if I was in the bunk room in the back of the boat house. Mom became frantic when she saw dad pale as a ghost and alone. By all accounts fifteen or twenty minutes had already elapsed. They ran outside and began searching the water and saw the blanket floating in the oily harbor water. Dad dove in boots and all, ruining his watch and a pack of Camels as he searched for me.

When he surfaced a crowd of sailors had gathered with a line and flotation devices to pull us from the water. Someone called 911 and I don't remember but mom or dad performed cpr. I was blue they later told me. I was cold, still and lifeless. When the ambulance arrived I was still not conscious but the paramedics I am told were able to restore some breathing and a pulse. They could not keep me breathing however. I was rushed to the hospital we're I would remain to recover for a very long time. When I finally awoke my first words were "I'm thirsty" this was the happy ending to the whole affair, mom and dad delighted in telling that part of the story I would hear time and time again as I grew up.

The details might change but that's how I recall it, though I have no memory really other than an occasional waking nightmare probably more a product of the story than the event itself. For some unfathomable reason I have always been drawn to the sea. In the nightmare I am called to it by a dark and violent monster – a hideous yet featureless black being that I am powerless to resist- I relive a drowning experience and awake. When I awake

I try to remember it, to separate reality from illusion. I remember the sun glistening through the water above me, partly obscured by the blanket and the sharp rocks of the bottom against my skin.

My brain was damaged by the incident of course, and my constitution would suffer as I grew up. I could never match the strength and speed of the other children in my peer group. I suffered from several learning disabilities. I had developed a stutter; I would become dyslexic and suffer seizures or unknown origin, and struggle to focus in school. This made me ripe for bullying. My father enrolled me in swimming and kung-fu lessons. I would do well enough to defend not only myself but I would frequently come to the aid of my sisters with the rudimentary skills and confidence I would gain. I would not participate in expensive formal classes for long though. I would practice what I could, researching forms from books in the school library or studying with friends who could afford formal classes. I would frequently dominate our informal contests because nothing else seemed to matter; I was destined to be a fighter.

Death in the Family

While I survived the drowning, death returned to our family to take a child about a year later. My mom had given birth to premature twins after a difficult pregnancy. The babies were not ready to breathe on their own and both were struggling, with neither expected to survive. After a week, one of the twins who had seemed to be recovering suddenly perished. The other twin, apparently the weaker of the two suddenly reversed and in almost no time was cleared to go home. It was a bittersweet moment for our family that brings a tear to my eye as I remember it. And I do remember it, spending so much time in the hospital waiting areas, dad smoking a pack of cigarettes at a stretch standing watch over us in the waiting room (in the 70s you could smoke in hospitals).

The babies were named Melody and Marissa. Marissa was laid to rest in the family plot, which was later stolen from us by the unscrupulous company that operated the graveyard in one of the larger scandals of the kind to ever occur in Honolulu. Tens of millions of dollars stolen and properties lost. We visited Marissa frequently when we were young, I don't think I can find her grave site anymore.

She was the cutest baby, so tiny. But I have her twin for a little sister. Your aunt Melody is a kind and vibrant spirit. She is my closest relative; she knows me better than mom or our other sister. We've shared more misery and adventure with each other than with anyone. I miss my sister and home very much. Growing up she was always there tagging along with me and my friends. Right up through late in high school when she'd make pancakes for my buddies who were passed out in the front room after a hard night of marathon PlayStation. My friends adored her, and she is still in touch with some of my old high school chums.

Back to Today

Parenting isn't all near death experiences or accidents. It's mostly just diapers and runny noses, messes at meal times. I quipped just the other day that if you were to film a documentary of my life at home, you'd think I was a poop hobbyist. I spend a lot of time cleaning diapers, taking your sister to the potty and of course there is the cat box your pregnant mother can't clean.

But all of that is worth it to hear you kids running to greet me in the kitchen when I come home at night. I like to read stories to each of you, Miranda doesn't have a favorite and won't always sit still for a story and you won't go to bed unless I read *Goodnight Moon* every night. I love the smiles and laughs that I get in response to dumb jokes I make that no one else would laugh at. I like watching you discover new things that are old hat to me. A couple of nights ago I made hot chocolate for you and your sister for the first time with milk and Swiss Miss Mix. You kids loved that and behaved for the rest of the evening too busy slurping cocoa to do anything naughty. Watching you learn is also great fun. This week you've learned to put your pajamas shirt on. Your sister mastered the sleeves before you did. She excels at physical gross motor skills.

Holidays like Christmas are fun too. Your mother and I built a jungle gym in the play room for you and now I have to disassemble it to move it into the yard. This year was also the first time you sat on Santa's lap. Last year you were too afraid of him. Santa was in the town square at the "Santa Shanty" I wonder if it'll still be there when you have kids. Christmas is fun without kids yes, but it's really better with them. Enjoy it as best you can with your own children, it's all going by too fast for your mother and I.

Chapter 11

Uncertainty

"Although our intellect always longs for clarity and certainty, our nature often finds uncertainty fascinating."

-Karl Von Clausewitz

Surprisingly I was surprised to find the universe still so full of surprises. I shouldn't have been surprised, I had spent most of my life struggling and usually failing to purge insecurity and uncertainty from my world. The foundation my family had given me was quicksand that caused me to be a bit nervous and fearful. My early career was a false start and characterized by temporary, seasonal or intermittent work. I was trapped in perpetual motion, admittedly sometimes caused by my own restlessness. For example, I decided to go to Bosnia in an afternoon, with only two weeks to prepare.

I dislike surprises and unexpectedly being at someone else's mercy so I tried to choose my own beginnings and the time for my exit from a situation. I enjoyed a sense of power over my own life when I could. When people asked me about this swashbuckling lifestyle I replied that "life is too short to do just one thing forever and I was out there experiencing everything I could." Some people suggested my bouncing around was extreme, I tell them "my earliest memory is a near death experience so for me each day is a gift. I have been given a second chance at tomorrows that are never guaranteed." I am determined to cram all the stories and adventures that could be crammed into ten lifetimes. I will not die wondering what might have been.

When I would have a new beginning someplace I would have to start over with regards to establishing seniority and trust. I would have to establish new social networks, which increases in difficulty with age. If tough jobs or choice assignments were available I would usually miss the latter and get stuck with the former. On the upside those tough jobs gave me a chance to prove my quality to my new circles. I spent most of my time as an outsider, which meant that I was able to indulge my favorite pastime: reading. Being an outside also meant I learned to sense or hear what people were thinking. It was an adaptation I had to obtain to quickly acclimate to new social environments and to integrate into the circles and cliques I would need to move through to be comfortable or effective. When I met your mother I was resigned to drift for the rest of my life.

Then there she was, and she quickly changed my outlook. Initially she and I indulged in a little adventuring together, each of us eager to reclaim our right to happiness and make up for some time lost on losers that repressed us. We settled down just before you were born, we tossed out the anchor and bought the hundred year old house. I thought I had a good handle on things. I guess I was a bit overconfident about my abilities, which had served me well and that as much as anything contributed to my surprise. Personally, I had been able to get out in front of things for a while and thought I could continue doing that without trouble. With regards to parenting I had changed a diaper or two before when my sisters were new and I could remember enough of my helping to raise them that I could handle anything a ten pound baby could throw at me.

Or so I thought. Honestly I'm glad I was wrong. Most of the surprises life has thrown at me were welcome ones, delightful and joyous. As things settled down I wasn't disappointed, I was proud that I had been able to achieve some kind of stability important for a family. I wanted the children to have something more than a foundation of quicksand from which to embark upon their own journey. I know now there is no reason to fear uncertainty, I wish I had known that before. Still, it's prudent to prepare for some contingencies and to be flexible, ready to respond and adaptive. You want your family to enjoy a sense of security and stability, you shouldn't fear uncertainty but because kids do you should do your best to keep disruptions to a minimum for their sake.

A key time to avoid disrupting a routine or creating anxiety about change is the birth of a baby. If at all possible, when expecting a baby avoid changing jobs, or moving to a new town. If you move to a more secure setting, a safer or larger one, that might makes sense but do it early. If you're going to consider a job, make sure it's a step up and don't neglect to consider the benefits. Kids are always at the doctors and accidents like drowning happen, which can be expensive. Not to mention what it costs to have a baby. I was lucky I was in the Air Force when you were born and they paid for everything except the cost of the TV and phone in the hospital room. Most jobs don't come with this kind of benefit. My Commerce Department job fortunately did provide a similar benefit for Miranda's birth.

I'm lucky, we're lucky that we enjoy a good deal of security but sometimes that's an illusion. People often equate the military and government work with security but in my time I've been downsized out of a military unit and my government agency is cutting personnel, more than twenty from my 130 man department in the first round of cuts announced. I figure the best thing I can do to be prepared is to be flexible and continue learning so that I remain marketable, prepared to land on my feet. With kids depending on you, you'll have to find a way to do that, it's what dad's do. Have a plan "B", another skill set, a marketable hobby and boldly go forward. Fortune favors the bold and prepared mind.

I want to share the worst situation I was in that caused uncertainty for me. To learn and gain wisdom, you shed some illusions of youth. I thought the military was a meritocracy with morality and honor foremost in importance. Turns out these things are usually just paid lip service to in the military and government, particularly amongst the officer corps. Those guys run everything and act like business men or politicians. Particularly in intelligence where our craft is deception which creeps in to everyone's personality – we are what we do aren't we? In intelligence we traffic in lies and that is not good for the soul. We rationalize unspeakable things and lose ourselves in the doing. So I discovered I was not a good fit for intelligence and the military in general. I endeavored to remain a man of conscience, and if I was to grow in rank I'd have to abandon that. It was a crisis of conscience that began simmering in Bosnia and came to a boil just a bit after you were born. It wasn't the best time to have an unstable situation. It didn't help that the Air Force had determined I was no longer needed either. I had to find a new job. Was it the universe speaking to me?

After years of soldiering I was being cut. There was a chance though to stay and fight for a position in the 193rd Special Operations Wing, but I judged that battle unwinnable. It's important to know whether a fight can be won before becoming committed to it. Never join a battle you are not certain of winning, being committed without knowing the outcome is defeat. We'll talk about battles won, lost and avoided in the next chapter. If you find yourself in this situation I want you to know you can get through it, I did.

Don't worry, don't panic just put your head down and move forward. You'll do what you must do as a dad, if you doubt your ability to do so, which is natural, doubt will go away. When your kids want for something you'll know what to do. In the hundred year old house we had oil heat and that meant a huge bill of $400 or $500 dollars (roughly 1/3 of my bimonthly paychecks) could appear at any moment depending on how fast the furnace burned it which was driven by the weather. You can't get much more uncertain than the weather. I had to get creative with accounting, our supplier wouldn't take checks the first year, but we pulled through two winters in that situation. Your mother never knew how tight money was during those times. I was able to make it work and insulated her from worrying about it so she could focus on you and so you wouldn't sense her worry.

    Kids seem to be very empathic. Today you were sick and threw up for the first time. You were lethargic all day with a slightly elevated temperature. Your sister knew something was wrong and didn't pester you or pelt you with toys like she normally does, she gave you room to rest. You guys always know when I'm angry or tired too. Kids can sense stress, fear and worry so you want to do your best to keep that boogeyman at bay for them. That's what dads do. It's what we're here for.

    I had to adapt to uncertainty from an early age. I've come to accept it. When I was a little boy though, about your age around the time I drowned, I was fraught with anxiety over my dad's frequent and unpredictably long sailings. He would sometimes go to sea for weeks or be sent to work in another islands harbor for months on end. When he left me at the door I had no concept of time, so I would panic and cry for my daddy not knowing if he would be gone for the day or the rest of my life. My dad always left mom and me at home for an overnight or longer sailing. He didn't let us send him off from the pier, especially after my first sister had arrived and I drowned. This helped me I suppose since I was at home, a comfortable setting to help me cope with my anxiety. This also helped to preserve going to the pier as a positive experience.

    Whenever we went to the pier we knew dad would be coming home that night. We'd get to eat a fun dinner too like cheeseburgers from the Burger King drive thru or saimin noodles from the L&L diner. If we had extra money we'd go to Zippy's[28]. When money wasn't good, it might just be ketchup sandwiches or scrounged food from the tugboat galleys. If we were especially lucky dad would have some fresh fish caught on his trip home and we'd feast like kings on free fish dinners fried in too much butter or grilled whole. The only down side was my dad would gross us out by eating the fish eyes saying "that's the best part, you don't know what you're missing." That memory still makes me cringe.

---

[28] Zippy's is like a diner or a Denny's but with an Asian twist.

It was probably the best thing my dad could think of to do to make his absence less traumatic. Those special surprises dad would bring home are why I don't come home from a weekend away empty handed. You and Miranda get toys or cookies every time I have to be away. The first time I went away without you I brought you the Elmo Color Carnival book and the little brown horse stuffy. In my mind though the best thing dad could have done was to quit being a damn sailor! That's why when I decided I wanted kids I quit being a sailor (full time anyway). My dad probably disliked being away then as much as I do now. I hate to make a trip away from my family for work. I just went to war with the Navy to reassign me closer to home so I could serve my part time commitment without disrupting our family quite so much as I've had to do lately.

I can't fault dad though for doing what he knew, he was not flexible or adaptable. He had not completed high school and had no realistic options. Men of his time didn't switch jobs or employers. When he was nearly killed by that anchor chain, I was happy to learn he would not be sailing again, to know he would never leave again. He was in the hospital a good few weeks within bicycle range of our house so I could ride my bike to see him anytime I wanted to while he recovered. During his extensive stay he got a blood clot and suffered a massive near fatal stroke. He had a five way bypass and was given only eighteen months to live (why do they tell kids this kind of stuff?). He went on ticking, through a few more strokes for more than fifteen years. Damn, he was tough.

You never know when something like that will happen. My dad had braved vicious storms, sailed in trouble waters, and been in WWII, Korea and Vietnam. All of a sudden on a calm sunny day working alongside a routine tourist loaded cruise ship an anchor chain parted sending several tons of iron hurtling towards his tiny harbor tug. That enormous shot of chain smashed the boat's superstructure as well as my dad's leg (the tug was never the same again and was retired). Poor dad was too tough to lose consciousness. Despite the shock, the compound open fracture and massive blood loss he remained cogent, directing his own rescue from the mangled boat or so the story goes. Two of the guys I sailed with some twenty years later were there that day and told it just the same way when welcoming me to their crew in the fall of 1997.

I count myself lucky, enduring uncertainty is about the worst sacrifice I've had to make for my career. During a tenure punctuated by continual war I've not suffered any great separations from my family, nor permanent injury or disability. Others who have served much less time have lost much more. Most of our current wars dead are barely out of their teens. Too young to even understand what was happening around them. I've been lucky that most of my surprises have been good ones. This is not to say that the burden of uncertainty has always been easy. Not knowing where I would work or if I should fight for my job in 2009 landed me in the hospital briefly with an irregular heartbeat. That year probably aged me two or three. I've certainly gotten more grey hairs since that late 2008, early 2009 period (though I still have a good deal less than Alvie). That period was full of skirmishes and struggles, some of my toughest times. I am a warrior in spirit and profession, and though I wish another way for my children I will devote the next chapter to that topic entirely instead of hinting at or dancing around it as I have in previous sections.

Chapter 12

Of War and Battles

"I must study politics and war that my sons may have liberty to study mathematics and philosophy."

-John Adams, Founding Father, 2nd U.S. President

Externally, sometimes bold decisions lead to conflict. Making decisions in the face of opposition or uncertainty almost necessarily mean some obstacle, usually defended by a rival or adversary must be overcome. Sometimes you are that obstacle for someone else, just being a man of honor can make you a problem for less scrupulous people. Sometimes it is enough to be different, the "hated other" to find yourself in a fight. I'll talk about the dangers of speaking truth to power here, one of the tougher fights you might find yourself in. I'll use John Boyd's challenge and a second story about Colonel Arthur L. Wagner to illustrate this.

Internally, unrealistic expectations, loss of illusions, desires, pride, uncertainty and fear will cause tumult. Your own heart and mind will make you your own worst enemy. These battles to conquer the self and master your own passions will be the hardest battles. You won't win all of these. You will fight them over and over all your life. Be prepared to settle for a draw. I'll only briefly discuss my battles with the Navy and 193rd here and how these ultimately were battles "won" within. Your mother fought these at my side and they might not have been won without her. You'll have to analyze incidents throughout to get a sense of how conflicted some of the decisions in my life were. I think it's fairly apparent so I won't spend too much time on this here.

When forced into a fight, get help. Don't expect to win if you fight alone. Even internal battles can benefit from the help of a loved one or close friend to advise you. A confidant always helps make bearing the burden easier and can help you find the way out of the worst tangled mess. As I said you mother was there to help me, and I needed her. In other battles with a light colonel I didn't like, I had Alvie. With his help I learned the hard lesson that people hate to hear "no" and I learned how to keep saying it anyway.

Colonel Boyd

I had included Boyd in Chapter 3 as one of my heroes. Many others could have been included but Boyd made the final cut for a number of reasons. Like me, his work was in the background as a trainer and teacher, a researcher and thinker. He contributed in a supporting role. He was bombastic and famous for lengthy rants. Alvie and any of my bosses will say I share that quality with Boyd. He is known to take some creative license with his story telling, as I do to make a point. His best is setting fire to a hangar once as a junior airman. My best story has something to do with a fire as well. The most important reason Boyd was selected is for his universal applicability. His lessons are applicable in any conflict and worth reading even if you never enter the profession of arms. Col. Boyd's work is preserved and built upon by a number of researchers and fans who are alive and carrying on his work[29] advocating for reform in national defense.

Though Boyd associated with many junior officers during his Air Force career, there were a few, perhaps half a dozen, that he had such respect for that he invited them to join him on his quest for change. Each one would be offered the choice: Be someone - be recognized by the system and promoted - or do something that would last for the Air Force and the country. It was unfortunate, and says something about the state of American's armed forces[30], that it was rarely possible to do both.

Boyd's biographer, Robert Coram, collected the invitation from an officer who got it and selected the "to do" option, and he confirmed its essence from several others.

"Tiger, one day you will come to a fork in the road," he said. *"And you're going to have to make a decision about which direction you want to go."* He raised his hand and pointed. *"If you go that way you can be somebody. You will have to make compromises and you will have to turn your back on your*

---

[29] Available through the Defense and the National Interest or DNI website www.dnipogo.org.
[30] Even in the 1950s and 60s it was getting bad.

friends. But you will be a member of the club and you will get promoted and you will get good assignments." Then Boyd raised his other hand and pointed another direction. "Or you can go that way and you can do something – something for your country and for your Air Force and for yourself. If you decide you want to do something, you may not get promoted and you may not get the good assignments and you certainly will not be a favorite of your superiors. But you won't have to compromise yourself. You will be true to your friends and to yourself. And your work might make a difference." He paused and stared into the officer's eyes and heart. "To be somebody or to do something. In life there is often a roll call. That's when you will have to make a decision. To be or to do. Which way will you go?[31]

Colonel Boyd's experience being denied promotions and his invitation is illustrated by what happened to Colonel Wagner at the outset of the Spanish-American War. Wagner demonstrates an important principle in life as well as war where mistakes equate to death and can mean the destruction of the nation-state.

At the outset of the Spanish-American War, Colonel Arthur L. Wagner was head of the Military Information Division (the War Department's embryonic intelligence organization). Driven by public sentiment, President McKinley and Secretary of War Russell A. Alger were determined to attack Spanish forces in Cuba not later than summer 1898. Wagner at once prepared a careful assessment of the Spanish forces, terrain, climate and environmental conditions in Cuba – the basic intelligence needed for operational planning. Wagner's assessment also identified recurring outbreaks of yellow fever in Cuba during the summer months as a crucial planning consideration. At a White House meeting, Wagner recommended postponement of any invasion until the winter months in order to reduce what would otherwise be heavy American losses from the disease. President McKinley reluctantly endorsed his view. As they left the meeting, Secretary of War Alger was furious with Colonel Wagner. "You have made it impossible for my plan of campaign to be carried out," he told Wagner. "I will see to it that you do not receive any promotions in the Army in the future." The Secretary of War made good on his promise, for although Colonel Wagner was promoted years later to brigadier general, the notice of his appointment reached him on his death bed. Furthermore, Alger influenced McKinley to reauthorize a summer invasion of Cuba. Fortunately United States forces won a quick victory, but as Wagner predicted, the effects of disease soon devastated the force. The ravages of yellow fever, typhoid, malaria and dysentery accounted for more than 85 percent of total casualties and were so severe that by August 1898 less than one quarter of the invasion force

---

[31] From *Boyd: the fighter pilot who changed the art of war* by Robert Coram.

remained fit for service. According to his peers, Wagner deliberately jeopardized his career in order to satisfy a sense of duty, rather than bow to political pressure. Information that American lives could be saved by avoiding the worst time of the year for yellow fever was more important to him than currying favor with the Secretary of War. [32]

My own battles like these are governed by non-disclosure agreements or highly classified and cannot be shared until after my death. They are not as noteworthy as Colonel Wagner's but were not less difficult or isolating and costly for a Sergeant. Today I defend a nuclear reactor facility as the lone keeper of "no" near our nation's capital, as our country is dragged by a runaway train towards war with Iran. My facility sits in a county with the second highest concentration of Iranian nationals in the U.S. But I can talk about the internal and human resources battles I've fought and about war in general.

War

"All war is deception"

– Sun Tzu

In modern war too much of this deception is directed against the people of the state whose ruling elite wish to take to war. I've learned over the course of my career that our country has been continually at war, usually covertly, in at least a handful of places at any given time. Our government seems to be little more than a provider of military forces for global banking cabals bent on overthrowing every nation that doesn't swear allegiance to or at least cooperate with their own banking regime.

Today their sites are set on Iran, and recently some propagandists have been trying to convince our government to take us into Uganda to fight a guy who isn't even there anymore, to prop up a pro west dictator over the country where coincidentally we've discovered oil and mineral deposits worth untold dollars. The state department or another group of administration puppets will provide some ridiculous rational for attacking or invading. Right now with Iran it's the same discredited argument they used in Iraq: weapons of mass destruction and ties to al-Qaeda. There will be a new bad-guy du jour when you're of age for military service. Unless someone invades Pennsylvania or a neighboring state, there isn't a good reason to wear a uniform for a living as I have. In the event you discard this refrain you'll need to know a few things going in.

---

[32] Excerpted from the J-2 Doctrinal Document www.dod.gov/pubs

Principles of War

"War is something absurd, useless, that nothing can justify"

-Louis de Cazenave, French WWI Veteran

Karl Von Clausewitz gives us the basis of the modern U.S. Principles of War[33]. Failure to consider these principles in planning and execution will lead to failure. This information would be of use to you as a senior NCO, an analyst or office, even a civilian in the CIA or other defense oriented analytics contractor. There are rumblings about adding Flexibility to this list but modern management practices, a zero defects mentality resulting in risk aversion and micromanagement enabled by information technology make this increasingly unlikely.

Study of Operational Art, particularly as practiced by the Germans (since before Hitler & "Blitzkrieg") is of particular value to understand how to link the levels of war flexibly. The U.S. is a C- student in Operational Art, graded on a bell curve with Russia and Germany at opposite extremes. If you are placed in command and implicit orders aren't available keep in mind two things 1) Enemy commanders (specifically German Field Marshall E. Rommel) have complained that U.S. forces are successful precisely because they don't follow their own doctrine and 2) it's easier to get forgiveness than permission, especially if you're begging it from atop a hard won objective (something General G.S. Patton might have said). So go forward, go boldly, go now and go guns ablaze.

Clausewitz's principles expanded upon and modified by others since his day are now generally ordered thusly:

Objective – Direct every military operation toward a *clearly defined*, decisive and *attainable* objective. The ultimate military purpose of war is the *destruction* of the enemy's *ability* to fight and *will* to fight.

Offensive – Seize, retain, and *exploit* the initiative. Offensive action is the most effective and decisive way to attain a clearly defined common objective. Offensive operations are the means by which a military force seizes and holds the initiative while maintaining freedom of action and achieving decisive results. This is fundamentally true across all levels of war.

---

[33] Reference U.S. Army Field Manual FM 3-0, the U.S. isn't the best place to learn military art.

Mass – Mass the *effects* of overwhelming combat power at the decisive place and time. Synchronizing all the elements of combat power where they will have decisive effect on an enemy force in a short period of time is to achieve mass. Massing effects, rather than concentrating forces, can enable numerically inferior forces to achieve decisive results, while limiting exposure to enemy fire.

Economy of Force – Employ all combat power available in the most effective way possible; allocate minimum essential combat power to secondary efforts. Economy of force is the judicious employment and distribution of forces. *No part of the force should ever be left without purpose.* The allocation of available combat power to such tasks as limited attacks, defense, delays, deception, or even retrograde operations is measured in order to achieve mass elsewhere at the decisive point and time on the battlefield.

Maneuver – Place the enemy in a position of disadvantage through the flexible application of combat power. Maneuver is the *movement* of forces in relation to the enemy to gain positional advantage. Effective maneuver keeps the enemy off balance and protects the force. It is used to exploit successes, to preserve freedom of action, and to reduce vulnerability. It continually poses new problems for the enemy by rendering his actions ineffective, eventually leading to defeat.

Unity of Command – For every objective, seek unity of command and unity of effort. At all levels of war, employment of military forces in a manner that masses combat power toward a common objective requires unity of command and unity of effort. Unity of command means that all the forces are under *one* responsible commander. It requires a single commander with the requisite authority to direct all forces in pursuit of a unified purpose.

Security – Never permit the enemy to acquire unexpected advantage. Security enhances freedom of action by reducing vulnerability to hostile acts, influence, or surprise. Security results from the measures taken by a commander to protect his forces. Knowledge and *understanding* of *enemy* strategy, tactics, doctrine, and staff planning improve the detailed planning of adequate security measures.

Surprise – Strike the enemy at a time or place or in a manner for which he is unprepared. Surprise can decisively shift the balance of combat power. By seeking surprise, forces can achieve success well out of proportion to the effort expended. Surprise can be in tempo, size of force, direction or location of main effort, and *timing*. Deception can aid the probability of achieving surprise.

Simplicity – Prepare clear, uncomplicated plans and concise orders to ensure thorough understanding. *Everything in war is very simple*, but the simple thing is difficult. To the uninitiated, military operations are not difficult. Simplicity contributes to successful operations. Simple plans and clear, concise orders minimize misunderstanding and confusion. Other factors being equal, parsimony is to be preferred.

History is replete with great stories of horrible battles where these lessons were learned and relearned at incredible, sometimes unbearable expense. When facing Operation Overlord Hitler was convinced that Patton would attack at Pa de Calais and held his heavy armor in reserve awaiting his invasion. This allowed the Allied forces to attack and secure Normandy beaches despite being unable to land heavy armor in quantity and numerous other problems. The allied infantry was able to hold on within striking distance of enemy armor. This illustrates surprise, security and maneuver at work as well as the importance of knowing your enemy as discussed in the next section on Sun Tzu.

An important factor, surprise is sometimes misunderstood. Napoleon once said[34] that "uncertainty is the essence of war, surprise its rule." Pearl Harbor demonstrates a problem that can result from surprise that is worth observing. Through history surprise attacks have often only angered the victims of the dastardly attack bringing doom on the attacker. On that strategic level[35] surprise often provides poor results for the attackers. From the simmering debate on the utility of surprise and Sun Tzu's and Clausewitz's differences on the topic know this: Tactically it is indispensable and ever present, strategically it's near impossible to achieve and potentially counterproductive.

Unity of Effort and Command are frequently problematic, if not ignored by those who seek to cultivate massive staffs and complex command networks as a status symbol. It can create problems and cost lives. These commanders frequently ignore simplicity as well. The worst offense however is our military commander in chief – the President and the civilian Congress. They ignore the very first and most important principle – Objective. Our military is bogged down all over the world, in Afghanistan most visibly and

---

[34] Handel, "Intelligence and the problem of strategic surprise"
[35] The three levels of war are strategic (global) operational (theatre/regional) tactical (close quarters/walking distance)

no one can really say why or what we're trying to achieve there in any concise or sensible way.

Back to the tactical level of war though where death is found, amongst the gravel and weeds of war's dirty tasks. Here you will find surprise and initiative the ruling principles. Initiative is the ability to decide your actions. If you are fighting from a static position, unable to maneuver you cannot control the flow of operations and the enemy is said to have the initiative, he can pick his place and time of attack while you sit waiting. Our doctrine can limit our ability to keep the initiative; logistics can threaten it once attained. For example, certain enemies know we don't leave wounded on the field, we send medics and aides to them. This means for each U.S. Soldier you wound, you take three or four out of the fight. Knowing this they plan their attacks to spread injuries, not necessarily lethal wounds, across an area. This stops U.S. units in their positions as they'll turn to tending their injured instead of pressing an attack. Our doctrine of "no man left behind" is a tactical, if ethically necessary, hindrance to maintaining the initiative and attaining objectives.

If you are moving and gaining ground on an adversary and your tank runs out of gas, it becomes static and a tank is nearly useless in defense so you lose the initiative here as well. The enemy can run or attack in a way best to his advantage, or bypass your position all together. You lose the initiative. Through history one of our greatest advantages has been logistics; don't neglect this in planning should you find yourself in a position to influence operational planning in whatever war you're in. Losing the initiative is often fatal.

Another important principle of maneuver is to move forward through the enemy. Battle experience has shown that enemy troops fire further away as a battle wears on, becoming less accurate and effective in close. Historically attempting to flee or break contact is when the slaughters occur. Yield in response to a surprise offense or thrust but don't turn your back; side step or step back. Withdraw under cover and with control but don't *run* away.

This brings me to Sun Tzu and the *Art of War*. This book is often misquoted and misunderstood. One of the most frequently quoted lines is key in all competitive human endeavors, you can be certain Peyton Manning knows it.

> *"If you know your enemies and know yourself, you can win a hundred battles without a single loss. If you only know yourself, but not your opponent, you may*

win or may lose. If you know neither yourself nor your enemy, you will always endanger yourself."

The book successfully spans the strategic and tactical levels of war. Some of the meanings are difficult to understand without knowing ancient Chinese infantry tactical terminology. This contributes to ongoing debate over the meanings of his terrains and elements amongst scholars. Nonetheless it is a critical work to review regularly. Hackworth preached reading a chapter each day (they are short having been written on bamboo originally) because understanding can be improved with repeated visits to the text. If you end up in the military before I die, you'll receive a good copy of this work with some further notes from me (and at least one Hackworth book). The book is also something I'd be happy to discuss with you at any time. A brief summary of the chapters follow keeping in mind modern translations with discussion are thick tomes:

> Laying Plans - explores the five fundamental factors and seven elements that determine the outcomes of military engagements. By thinking, assessing and comparing these points, a commander can calculate his chances of victory. Habitual *deviation* from these calculations *will ensure failure* via improper action. The text stresses that war is a very grave matter for the state, and must not be commenced without due consideration.

> Waging War - explains how to understand the economy of warfare, and how success requires *winning* decisive engagements *quickly*. This section advises that successful military campaigns require limiting the cost of competition and conflict.

> Attack by Stratagem - defines the source of strength as *unity*, not size, and discusses the five factors that are needed to succeed in any war.

> Tactical Dispositions - explains the importance of defending existing positions until a commander is capable of *advancing* from those positions in safety. It teaches commanders the importance of *recognizing* strategic *opportunities*, and teaches not to create opportunities for the enemy.

> Energy - explains the use of creativity and *timing* in building an army's momentum.

> Weak Points & Strong - explains how an army's opportunities come from the openings in the environment caused by the relative weakness of the enemy in a given area.

Maneuvering The Force - explains the dangers of direct conflict and how to win those confrontations when they are forced upon the commander.

Variation in Tactics - focuses on the need for *flexibility* in an army's responses. It explains how to respond to *shifting circumstances* successfully.

The Army on the March - describes the different situations in which an army finds itself as it moves through new enemy territories, and how to respond to these situations. Much of this section focuses on *evaluating* the *intentions* of others.

Terrain - looks at the three general areas of resistance and the six types of ground positions that arise from them. Each of these six field positions offer certain advantages and disadvantages.

The Nine Situations - describes the nine common situations (or stages) in a campaign, from *scattering* to *deadly*, and the specific focus that a commander will need in order to successfully navigate them.

The Attack by Fire - explains the general use of weapons and the specific use of the *environment as a weapon*. This section examines the five targets for attack, the five types of environmental attack, and the appropriate responses to such attacks.

The Use of Spies - focuses on the importance of developing good information sources, and specifies the five types of intelligence sources and how to best manage each of them.

You can see immediately similarities between the Clausewitz principles and some of Sun Tzu's key concepts. Sun Tzu's work is more tactically focused and deals heavily with disposition and employment of forces specifically while Clausewitz discusses planning for large campaigns and considers the political ramifications and costs of war as well. Clausewitz's book, *On War* was finished by his wife and might not be a properly complete work. Clausewitz never saw combat, but Sun Tzu is said to have lead troops on the field and killed with his own sword. Which do you think is more important to know?[36]

I would recommend Hackworth and Boyd's writings which show the application of these ancient texts in a more contemporary context. By your time there will be others.

---

[36] Answer: which ever most closely reflects the thinking of your enemy.

HR and Other Evils

"Boss your boss just as soon as you can. There is nothing he will like so well, if he is the right kind of boss. If he is not, he is not the man for you to remain with. Leave him whenever you can, even at a present sacrifice, and find one capable of discerning genius"

-Andrew Carnegie

And so we come to the more difficult battles, those won outside the battlefield. Human Resources decisions miscommunicated or hidden by leadership has been a source of many frustrating battles in my life. Disbanding of the 628th Military Intelligence Battalion left me searching for a new home. I was unable to conquer fear and move out beyond the military and counted myself lucky to have found a home with the Air Force, but my situation did not improve. Later I was downsized by the Air Force but management decided to hide this from me and they played games with my career until one of their favorites was in a position to promote past me.

That girl, who had less than half my time in service and no combat experience was of the same race and religion as the leadership. She attended the same college as the commander and everyone suspected she was sleeping with the E-9. I was tolerated because I was effective and efficient, but as soon as I challenged this favorite girl for a promotion I was suddenly downsized and not promotable. I had known that my position was eliminated some time ago (thanks to Alvie) and maintained by bureaucratic trickery only because I kept the leadership from having to find a replacement or shift the burden of my workload onto someone else.

I mounted a brief challenge to leadership because I only had to change positions to be eligible for promotion but decided to withdraw. Even if I took the promotion it wasn't where I wanted to be long term. I fought against myself and my own rage to walk away. I was lucky again to find a better paying job in short order. My sudden departure was an embarrassment for the commander who was soon after released. I had to overcome myself to do the smart and ultimately right thing for the family and avoid a battle that could not be won against bosses not worth working for. I still couldn't walk completely away from the uniform though. I ended up in the Navy and soon walked into another battle.

After being marginalized by the chain of command and denied a promotion or the right to compete for it for years on end, I discovered that they had been allowing others to apply though I was superior, and they didn't meet requirements I was being told I had to meet. I sought advice and considered the costs carefully before deciding to engage. After a year of battle with the Navy, including intervention of Congressman Platts on my behalf, I obtained a favorable outcome. The Navy wouldn't admit wrongdoing but dropped its opposition to a desirable transfer, allowed me to backdate my promotion and to keep my bonus. I was able to obtain an apology from a junior officer who corroborated my complaint, though the Navy continues to deny any wrong doing.

Today, after just a single training meeting with that unit I find myself in another difficult battle with myself. The Seabee unit I have been attached to as the intelligence officer has some enlisted personnel involved in an academic cheating ring. I have been given a number of answer keys by the units career counselor which I am told are the correct answers for a number of Navy correspondence courses. Bringing the truth to the attention of the Navy hasn't helped me before and I have only just arrived at the unit so I am loathe to rock the boat as it were, which will likely result only in me being transferred yet again.

It seems that my interest in continuing my career might best be served by quietly ignoring this. I have no information on who exactly benefited from the cheating or how. I'm anxious to avoid further controversy in my career; these last two years have been very contentious. I wrestle with what to do about this. I may not decide by the time this is completed and there is no rush to act, delaying could result in discovering further information that could bear on the decision. Is this a hill I am willing to die on? What is the benefit of engaging in this fight? What will be lost if I don't engage?

Conclusion

"Only the dead have seen the end of war"

-George Santayana

If this section seems disproportionally longer than the others, war is what I do, it's what I know the most about. And if God forbid you find yourself in the army, then this is the perhaps the most important chapter. I hope it can help you. If you take only one thing away from this lesson let it be this: **Don't panic**, think *as you do!* Maneuver for advantage, yield ground to deplete your enemies' energy, let his quick success surprise him, unbalance him and give him false confidence then kill him. War is a complex endeavor, I can't hope to give you more than a brief introduction to a few key ideas as my own limited knowledge took more than a decade to acquire and could fill ten books ten times the size of this one. You'll have to study and learn quickly to survive your wars. You will notice that in the writings of Sun Tzu, Clausewitz, Boyd or Hackworth no one mentions selfish careerism, mistreatment of your troops or personal glory seeking as a key to victory.

Some other practical items that can help you I will provide here:

Keep your head down and on a swivel.

Check and recheck your kit before leaving your base.

If things seem hopeless remember there is always (at least) one more thing you can do!

Have a go to hell plan (plan B) and recognize the enemy has a vote; contact with the enemy will always change everything so be prepared to adapt your plan.

In advance of battle, reconnoiter your objective, by map and in person if possible before you move on it.[37]

Expect everything may fail: communications, batteries, ammunition and vehicles. Certainly air cover will often fail to arrive or be effective when it does.

Supply lines get attacked, cache batteries, toilet paper, ammo and water.

Weapons break, be ready for it don't let that surprise you and cost a split second that can mean all the difference.

In close battle, blood is slippery on a bare floor and on weapons handles. Not so much in dirt, but it is slippery on grass.

You can break a rifle in melee combat and a knife thrust into a foe will stick. It takes some force to extricate a blade from a body, be ready for that.

There is nothing I can tell you to prepare you for the shock of the smell and gore, the screams of the dying or your body's own reaction to the shock of action.

---

[37] This is important for job interviews too; take some time to travel to the actual place so you know the time and route which will make getting there on time (15 minutes early) easier the next morning.

If you have to give someone CPR, you'll break their ribs but it could save them. Don't let that cracking sound stop you from trying it but be prepared for it not to work. Unlike TV, in real life CPR isn't a guarantee. Be careful not to break the xiphoid or sternum however.

If you knock someone unconscious in a fight, unless you actually killed them they'll only be out for a few seconds, in real life that only lasts 5-20 seconds or so, people don't stay "knocked out" for minutes or hours.

Speed is better than silence, you might be heard but the shock of speed can still create surprise.

With regards to battles with the self, or HR, ask yourself this question at the onset: is this the hill I want to die on? Any fight you engage in could be your last, figuratively or in a very real sense. My fight over the E-7 promotion briefly hospitalized me. It took a real toll on my health. If I pressed that fight, it might have killed me. Think about what is at stake, will a victory be worth it? What will defeat cost you? Ask yourself what you are trying to prove or hoping to gain in this fight. Sure someone might be doing something illegal but can you prove it and show harm caused to you? Who will listen or care? Who are your allies? Who are your enemies and their allies? You're might be better off walking away or ignoring it.

Lies are powerful things, your adversary will use them to protect their position and if they have allies your lonely truth will be dangerously outnumbered. Our integrity is not hurt by biding our time.

If none of this dissuades your from pursuing a career in warfare, perhaps this will. In all the excitement portrayed in film and literature one thing is usually neglected. The awful boredom of war. It drags on seemingly forever, and there are interminable waits for all kinds of mundane things. Tens of thousands of hours spent waiting for moments of sudden shock and terror that arrive without warning – a ship springs a leak, strikes a mine, or a fire erupts and cuts off power. A mortar shell explodes in your shower killing a guy on the crapper reading a magazine or some sniper shoots at you while you're trying to get your laundry. It's hell because it's boring. Mostly.

Act III Curtain

A Final Word

"My most brilliant achievement was my ability to be able to persuade my wife to marry me."

-Winston Churchill

You might expect some profound and wonderful thoughts here or some final explanation of my complete philosophy that has taken shape over the course of reviewing my life for this book. I had wondered myself what I might say except that this *is not* the final word. Of that I am sure. This is the end of this volume but all endings are also beginnings. In this case this will mark the place in time Volume II begins. But some reflections are in order so I will share a few thoughts.

Though my beginnings were humble and might easily have pointed to failure, I think I managed to do alright. I'm not rich or invited to fancy parties but I wouldn't be particularly comfortable maintaining excess wealth and I don't care for stuffy parties. I'm not a curmudgeon but I don't see a need to maintain excessive friendships or friends who might invite me to stuffy parties. I am a bottle of beer on the back porch or glass of wine on the couch kind of homebody now and I've always had few friends.

I nearly failed to escape my beginning. I was adrift in part waiting foolishly for a direction and in part doubting myself and fearing failure so intensely that I forgot how to dream. I found a start but I can't say it was because of courage or strength of character or anything but a simple moment of recognizing necessity. I was desperate to be something other than a statistic or a victim of my circumstance. I clawed my way out of hopelessness. All that was needed was the conscious effort to make a decision to make a beginning for myself, to take responsibility for my destiny. For you then I would say don't wait. Go. Make a *good enough plan*, it need not be perfect. Do not be afraid to fail, we all do. When you do, pick yourself up and start again.

Sadly my life would know little peace; I did not always know how to find it. I found myself in frequent conflicts, often for no good reason. I squandered my life in battles where winning often meant having to move on and begin again and I lost more often than not. I chose war as a profession and I regret that. For you perhaps practicing acceptance would be a wise lesson to take from my own costly wars. Know that *war is not the way* as I have learned.

Along the way I found the divine in people, art and nature where it had always been, had I only stopped to see it. I found hope and peace but it would be many years before I would begin to be at peace. Years before I could stop struggling and still my mind so that my heart could fill with contented joyfulness or just quiet. For you I would say worship or know the divine by daring to love many things. Seek out beauty and love, not enemies and war. Study math and philosophy as earnestly as I have war.

When your mother and I first met she observed I was very angry with my past that I had not yet reconciled. When my father died I was so angry with him I did not attend his funeral. I could have found a way to make the trip but I was so devastated by his loss I could not bear to see and know he was gone. His death had come before I was ready to lose him, before he had anointed me. He died without validating me. I hoped that if I did not go, did not see him in repose, he would live on. For you I hope you will not embrace hate or fear, harbor a grudge or struggle with validation. You will be a good man and you do not need me to validate you. Do good works and become good. Please do not wait until I am gone to sit and speak with me as men will speak to one another. I have many more stories to share.

For most of my life I foolishly sought adventure instead of seeing the beauty and joy in the adventures everyday could be. I had fallen victim to the propaganda of the war machines and the romance in adventure novels, failing to grasp the lessons. For you I would say, work towards your dreams, there will be ample adventures along the way, many will surprise you. Many of the adventures I found ended painfully and I am no better for having endured most of them.

I also weakened or severed ties to family isolating myself. For you, I ask for you to stay in touch, especially with your siblings. Your poor mother has none and is afraid she'll be alone once her parents are gone. I have siblings but I haven't seen them since before you were born and that's not right.

The Ox and Scorpio

And again, I struggled to find peace all my life. It didn't start to come together until you and your mother came into my life. It didn't have to take that long, I knew better but lacked the wisdom to put into action these last words here that are not my own. If you ever find yourself in turmoil and nothing seems to help, open the back cover of this book to find the wise and famous words of Ralph Waldo Emerson chosen as much for myself as for you my son:

"Nothing can bring you peace but yourself."

ABOUT THE AUTHOR

Michael Chandler is a Navy Reservist and has worn our countries uniform for over fifteen years, primarily in intelligence and special operations commands. He has devoted his life to the stoic principle of service to the greater community. He currently works for the Department of Commerce. He is a supporter of the Adams County Soup Kitchen and the Sea Shepherd Conservation Society. He graduated with a Bachelor's of Arts degree from Bellevue University, Nebraska and a Master's Degree from Fort Hays State University, Kansas. He grew up in Hawaii but currently lives in Gettysburg, Pennsylvania with his wife and children who he enjoys giving all of his spare time.